The Secret of Crossings

The Secret of Crossings

Rhyd Wildermuth

ISBN: 979-8-9852028-3-0

Published by Ritona Press
3 rue de Wormeldange
Rodenbourg, L-6955 Luxembourg

Editing: Laurie Dietrich

For more information on our titles, please visit
ABeautifulResistance.com

Within

The Sacred and the Symptom

The announcement on the intercom began again. Our train was delayed another twenty minutes, and I looked at my husband to see how he met the news. He was too busy to care, though. He was shaking a high-tech vending machine as a young girl and her mother looked on hopefully.

Among the many reasons I'll adore this man until the end of our days are moments like this; the quick, charming transformation—from a pensive intellectual with aristocratic fashion sense into a dashing street hero—that is automatic for him when he sees someone in need. Suddenly he's all wry wit, his smile that of a rogue crusader and, before you blink, he's carrying some old woman's groceries, lifting heavy luggage off a train for a young woman, or wrestling with a vending machine.

We were traveling to Köln, in Germany, for a night. Thanks to the sales of my recent book, I had enough money to finally do what I'd always wanted to do for the man—take him on a trip somewhere interesting and pay for it all. He'd never had a man do this for him, as it's always been he who paid and took care of all the details. I was thrilled to do this for us. It felt well-timed, as I also needed distraction from too much thinking about the world.

I watched him shake the machine again, and I asked him what was happening. He pointed to a package of candy that had become stuck where the girl couldn't reach it. In the grand scheme of human suffering such things might seem trivial, yet I've always felt a deep, indescribable sense of sadness when witnessing such moments.

It's happened to everyone, I'm sure, most often when we're children. Something in a glass case draws our desire. We ask for coins from our parents, or search for them in our pockets and, following the instructions, we do everything we're supposed to do on our end of the transaction. The machine then fulfills its part of the bargain, delivering on its promise—until it doesn't.

The machine is unthinking, unfeeling. We cannot ask it why it lied, why it failed. It is stealing from us, and we cannot beg it to return what is now rightly ours. There is never anyone to call, even if there's a number printed somewhere. They won't answer, or if they do the best they'll offer you is a refund by mail. Worst of all, you look a fool and feel like one: Others around you (if there are others) shake their heads in sorrow. "That happens," they might say, or "There is nothing to be done." You feel you should have known better and tell yourself never to trust anything again.

The sight of my husband shaking that machine was a beautiful sight. He's not really the sort to shake anything, to apply brute force to a problem. He's too deft, and too aristocratic. But he was shaking it, and it was beautiful.

The sight pulled me from my thoughts for a moment. I had been thinking about a friend I had some twenty years ago. We were roommates for a little while. My fondest memory of her is the morning she walked unannounced into my bedroom. I was naked in bed with another man, both of us asleep after a very long night. In my memory there is champagne in the wine glass she hands to me, but maybe it was just sparkling mineral water. Either way, she was holding two glasses, and one was for me.

"Wake up, dear," she said, then turned on the radio in my bedroom so I could hear the news everyone else was hearing that morning on September 11th. "It's the apocalypse." She was such an elegant mess, always darkly funny, bitingly and charmingly insulting. Her insights bore the mark of morbid genius. She had a contagious misanthropy, yet somehow still seemed kind and compassionate.

While we lived together, she got pregnant. The father was the type of man I came to know and recognize too well in radical circles, the "sensitive dreamer" type who is always working on a "brilliant" project that will change the world. They never have jobs, are usually on some sort of disability scheme, yet they have all the computer or music equipment someone with an actual income would struggle to purchase. He got her pregnant, and then he moved in with us for a little while, setting up his music equipment in our living room.

He told her he didn't want to be a father. She was already a mother, having had a child when she was a teenager. The father of that child was caring for it with the help of his parents, and my roommate had visitation rights. The father of this child had no intention of doing anything except living off of her while he worked on a musical project he named, in honor of the baby, "Fetal Distress."

I kicked him out. She acted angry about this, but I don't think she really was.

There were other ways she acted that I realized later didn't reflect how she really felt. She talked openly and quite caustically about how excited she was to get rid of the "parasite" growing inside of her, and about her complicated scheme to do so. Because she couldn't afford the procedure, she'd hatched a plan to get funds from a Catholic pro-life agency to pay for the abortion, a big "fuck you" to the Christians.

I didn't realize until later that she'd gone to them because she'd actually wanted the child.

The other roommates and I were verbally supportive of whatever she decided to do, but none of us had the financial stability to back those words up with something tangible. The father was a useless waste of humanity, so no help would be coming from him, either. Things got difficult in the house. She had an ultrasound and taped a printout of the image to the refrigerator door in our kitchen. One day I found that ultrasound image taped to a metal coat hanger suspended over the toilet in our bathroom. I asked her if I could please move it, and she got quite angry. "You can't understand," she shouted. And she was absolutely right.

The hardest moment was when she decided she would abort the child. She kept two rats she'd rescued from someone who wasn't taking care of them, and true to her dark sense of humor she named them "War" and "Pestilence." Pestilence died of a cancer, but not before mating with War. War was pregnant while my friend was pregnant, then gave birth and killed her children a week later. Even more morbid was what the rat mother did with the corpses. She didn't eat them, but piled them up and climbed on top of them to try to escape from the cage.

So, my friend decided to do the same.

I was remembering all this on the platform, watching my husband try to shake a child's candy free from an uncaring and treacherous machine. I looked to the mother, whose face shone with the look of relief you can see on anyone who finds they don't have to solve a pressing problem alone. Help an old woman with one of her grocery bags, offer to guide lost tourists to their destination, pick up something someone just dropped and offer it back to them, and you'll see that expression, too.

Rarely do we speak of this in discussions about abortion. It's here that the American left in particular reveals itself to be utterly devoid of compassion or humanity, preferring to speak about vague principles rather than acknowledging the core horror of the situation. In my experience, very, very, very few women want to kill the child growing inside them. The women in my life who have aborted often speak of it with pain and regret, wishing there had been another option.

The right isn't any better, though at least it understands that mothers having children is crucial to the health of humanity. American Christians speak of motherhood as sacred but leave it at that, forgetting that the sacred makes demands on humanity, not the other way around. The left, on the other hand, can barely even say the word "mother" anymore without adding gender clarifications so that a very tiny and very psychologically fragile handful of people don't get offended.

The overturning of *Roe vs. Wade*, in the United States, was inevitable, as it was a right granted by judicial fiat rather than one wrested from the government by the people. While access to abortion was seen as a "victory" for US feminism, there was no connection between the Supreme Court's ruling and protests in the streets. Rights granted by the powerful—rather than extracted from them—are rights easily taken back, and it's doubtful the pathetic excuse for a left in the US will ever understand this. For the next decade or so we'll probably have to endure screeds and altercations about principles fully detached from the embodied existence those principles claim to describe.

Abortion, like many such things, is a treatment for a symptom but does nothing about the underlying condition. The most commonly cited reasons why women get abortions—poverty, lack of support from a partner, unstable or abusive relationship situations, the inability to care for another child, a likely end to university studies or a career—are all material conditions.

If you want to make abortion rare, make it possible for women to be mothers without a descent into abject poverty, without becoming trapped in abusive relationships, and without motherhood dealing a deathblow to any hopes of self-betterment. The right needs to hear this, of course, but so does the left, perhaps even more so because these are the things every leftist movement worth the name once saw as crucial principles.

Abortion has become a poor replacement for an actual politics of human thriving. Abortions have always happened and will always happen, but they've been quite rare until the last few decades. People have always tried to stop them, but they cannot be stopped. Witch hunts didn't stop abortion, and the overturning of *Roe vs. Wade* won't stop it either. But this is all beside the point: Abortion is a shitty and unfortunate solution to a symptom, not the disease itself.

What if we truly saw motherhood as sacred again? I don't mean this in the faux American Christian way, but rather in the pagan and animist sense. What if motherhood was so sacred that society felt obligated to support it? What if the acts of conceiving and giving birth as well as continuously mothering a child were seen as such holy things that we acknowledged a duty to make sure women who chose to do so never lacked for anything? And what if we also saw fatherhood as truly sacred? Of course, we'd have to see the act of sex itself as sacred again as well, and not just in the empty way that monotheists and social justice ideologists claim to.

The sacred demands things of us, demands ritual and veneration and, most terrifying of all, it demands duty, obligation, and boundaries. We've come to see this understanding as primitive or reactionary, to see ourselves as "liberated" from the power and consequences flowing out of the very magic of human creation itself. So, we have sex without obligation, fatherhood without duty, motherhood without support, and no politics yet exists that can do anything but argue about who's at fault and who should be elected to fix it all. We cannot talk about the sacred, and we increasingly lose the language with which to speak of it.

If motherhood were sacred, and if fatherhood were sacred, then so too would be other acts and other choices. These were the thoughts that came to me while watching my husband struggle with that vending machine and remembering my friend. I think it was because of the way he'd just naturally stepped in to help, like a father might, responding to some very ancient human drive no longer seen as noble or even useful by modern capitalism. He isn't a father, nor will he (or I) ever be, but there's no other way to describe the duty with which he approaches his role as godfather to two kids and uncle to two nephews—and his struggle with that damn vending machine—except "sacred."

That sense of the sacred—and the sense of duty that comes with it—is also missing from the arguments about gender and trans identity. Some form of gender or sexual variance has always existed in human groupings, and until now it was seen as a sacred variance. Being outside "the binary" was a rare and protected position, and along with its sacred nature came sacred roles and duties. What we in modern, secular language call "homosexual" or "trans" was once known by countless other names, and meant something more than mere self-identification and difference. Forgetting and fighting that knowledge is making this conversation a mess, and it will only get worse for everyone.

We cannot speak of motherhood or fatherhood as sacred because we cannot speak of men or women as sacred, nor of sex as sacred, nor of anything as sacred at all. So, we'll only ever be able to treat symptoms, and fight about what those treatments should look like and who should be allowed to get them.

My husband's strength didn't prevail against that machine, by the way. However, another coin fed to the automated monster forced it finally to let drop what it had so cruelly withheld from the child.

I watched her and her mother walk away, happy and relieved, and I felt that we might all, one day, figure this stuff out. We cannot fix everything, of course, and we never will. We can only make some things less difficult for each other, less burdensome, less crushing. Doing so is sacred, because that's how we humans have always survived.

The Fear of Falling

I live in a beautiful, rural area, a small valley in the gently upward-sloping foothills of the Ardennes. There is a train servicing a village 5 kilometers from me but otherwise, because I do not drive, I bike a lot. I bike to the gym, to the grocery store, to nearby streams, to the heads of forest trails, and to the train station if I'd like to go farther than my bike can easily take me.

As I write this, I'm nursing a painful skin wound on my knee, after an intense bike crash, and I'm thrilled about it.

I've ridden bikes for most of my life, and still find them to be one of the few really brilliant human inventions. You move by using your legs and feet, but faster, and balance upon a linear plane only because you are moving. It's like flying, but you are always on the ground, which is good because I'm terrified of heights.

I never thought much about my fear of heights until quite recently. It's not a particularly crippling phobia for me, since for the most part I avoid experiences where I might feel vertigo. I have no reason to visit skyscrapers, and I'm not very often on mountain cliffs, so overall I forget that I'm terrified.

I was reminded a few months ago, though. It was my birthday, and my sister—who had rented a house for a week in Switzerland—invited my partner and I to come celebrate. I'd never been before, and I love mountains, and we had nothing else planned, so my husband agreed to drive us.

Driving through Switzerland is as gorgeous as you probably imagine. The land slopes ever upward from the lower plains of Germany until you are suddenly surrounded by visions out of *The Lord of The Rings*. It's also much like traveling through the Rockies or the Cascades in the United States, with the exception that the slopes and vales are populated by ancient Swiss villages, rather than American strip-malls and fast-food chains.

The last hour of the trip we could see nothing, as we hit a snowstorm. My husband is an extremely cautious and patient driver, but the stress of being able to see nothing but white, and a vaguely visible line of asphalt, through the windshield almost broke him.

Regardless, we arrived. The next morning, my sister told me her plan—she would take me to an incredible, snowy forest and show me some breathtaking views.

She's a really good liar, by the way. Not the sort of person who tells falsehoods, but rather the sort who tells you exactly what you want to hear, in order to obscure something that she knows you will not want to.

I forgot this about her, so I blindly and enthusiastically got into the car with my partner as he followed her and her family into my worst nightmare.

I didn't even realize what she had planned when we arrived at the bottom of a series of alpine gondolas.

"Oh, those are crazy," I said, and turned my face to the forested mountains instead. "Which way to the forest?"

My sister looked at me nervously. "We need to take a gondola there. But it's short, I promise. We'll be there before you even realize it."

Panic set in, and I grabbed my husband's hand. "Oh. You didn't tell me..." I said to her, still forgetting how brilliantly manipulative she can be.

"You don't have to go. But I really want you to see this."

"You know I'm afraid of heights."

She nodded. "That's why I didn't tell you."

My husband, who at this point assumed he knew everything about me, looked startled. "Tu as vertige? But you're never afraid of anything..."

I nodded. "It's really bad."

I could tell he was wrestling with an ugly choice. He could stay on the ground with me and be disappointed, or he could try to cajole me into going up with them despite how much I obviously didn't want to. The thing is, I *did* want to go. More than anything. But I knew what would happen if I got into that gondola.

My two young nephews were with us. Neither of them has any fear of heights, but because they're kids and understand fear better than us adults ever do, they both started trying to reassure me. "It's scary but it's okay," said the youngest, and the eldest said "I was scared the first time too."

When you're a 44-year-old man who's lived on the streets, traveled to foreign places with just a few hundred dollars, a tent, and a backpack, survived a few fist fights, an attempted mugging at gunpoint, and all manner of political threats, having a 10-year-old and a 6-year-old tell you to not be afraid is pretty wild. So, I got in the gondola. I was shaking even before the doors closed. I shut my eyes, grabbed a pole with a white-knuckled grip, and tried really hard not to act out the panic I was feeling.

Then the gondola started moving, and the feeling got even worse.

And then it was over and, although I wanted to vomit, everything was okay. We had arrived on a snow-covered cliff full of pines, and though I couldn't see much, I thought the view would probably be worth the terror.

I sat down, smoked a cigarette. My sister approached, apologetically asking if I was okay.

"Yeah," I said, realizing at that moment that I would need to take the same gondola back down. "I think I can even survive doing that again."

"Really?" she asked.

"Is there another way down?"

"Yes, but it takes two hours. You think you could do another one?"

I nodded, and she looked relieved but still a bit nervous.

"What about...two more?"

I breathed in really hard. "Uh...why?"

She was silent a moment. "This isn't where we're going. There's one or two more. But they are shorter."

The full horror of what she'd done to me finally unveiled itself, and I looked around. This was just an interchange spot, not an actual destination. It was the equivalent of arriving at a station where you change trains and thinking that the platform was your ultimate goal.

"Oh fuck," I said. "Okay."

She was lying again. There were not one or two more gondola rides, but three more. She knows me well, though. She knew I wouldn't have done any of it if I'd known the truth. She also knew that I'd later thank her for lying to me, which I did.

Our ultimate destination was Piz Gloria, a pinnacle made famous (and renamed) by an old James Bond film. From the very top you can see visions otherwise visible only by plane, the entire world as snow-covered mountains and endless sky.

At those dizzying heights you see what only the birds ever see, and while I stood gripping tightly to a railing, I watched ravens play in the cold winds and thought about how fear still holds me back from such moments of raw existence.

The current theory on the fear of heights—which I think is an accurate one—is that it is an inborn trait. Studies on human infants and the infants of other mammals (including mountain goats) have shown they all exhibit this fear, a panic when the ground seems to fall away from them. Most of us lose this fear the same way we lose other fears: We experience the consequences of the thing we feared.

The fear of heights is actually the fear of falling and when we fall, we learn to stop being so afraid of it. A person with vertigo closes their eyes because their vision is giving them the sense they are falling or about to fall. The visual of extreme distance doesn't match the physical sense of balance (on the floor beneath your feet in a gondola, the stone underfoot on a cliffside, the concrete upon which you are standing when looking over a bridge). So, suddenly all sensory information seems untrustworthy.

A person who fell repeatedly as a child, however, learned early on that there are moments when the visual system is unreliable and only the internal sense of balance, relayed through the inner ear and the body itself, can be relied upon.

The more often you fall, the more you rely on the rest of your body to guide your balance, and so eventually you fall less. To get to such a point, however, you need to put yourself in positions where you might fall.

I was an overly cautious child. I rarely climbed trees because I knew I might fall and that might hurt. Though my parents were not particularly attentive, I understood from them that taking risks was a bad thing to do, and therefore I avoided risk. My childhood obedience and caution are why I am still (but less so) terrified of heights.

This is also why I rarely crash my bike, something I've been trying to change. Today, riding home from doing some shopping, I took a particular curve in the path very fast. My bike tires are a bit deflated, and I know that this means turning can sometimes go wrong at high speeds. But I kept going, realizing that I was very likely to lose control and go toppling right at the sharpest point of the curve.

And I did. It was a rather spectacular crash, and it hurt quite a bit, and then I started laughing.

I should have experienced such things, often, when I was younger. I should have fallen more, by which I mean I should have let myself risk falling more often. I didn't really know what this sort of crash felt like, how much it would hurt, and how completely okay I'd be afterwards.

I've been trying to apply this ethic of risk-taking to the rest of my life, too. The relationship I am in with the man I love is the riskiest relationship I've ever dared. I almost didn't go on a second date with him, despite how utterly enchanting and beautiful the first had been, because I was terrified of falling in love with someone like him and how much doing so might stretch everything I knew about myself.

There are many other places I'm learning to fall, as well. You cannot climb higher, you cannot see the world from greater heights, until you know what falling teaches, and what comes after.

The World Outside the Universe

Carl Schmitt has observed that all modern "secular" political institutions are thinly veiled continuations of theological ones. More simply, though we may think of ourselves as modern and post-religious, our political framework is still very much a Christian one. A historical example should help you understand this point. In the Middle Ages, in Europe, during the time when the Catholic Church had its strongest hold over the meaning frameworks of people there, the idea developed that you were either part of a "universal communion" of believers (the word "catholic" means universal, and "communion" here functions just like the word community), or you were outside it.

In other words, there were two sorts of people: believers and unbelievers.

Being part of the in-group meant that you were protected by certain laws and moral standards that did not apply to the rest of the world. For instance, because slavery was a sin, a Catholic person could not be enslaved, although non-Catholics could be. Slavery—a form found almost universally, throughout history—was actually quite rare in most of Europe after the fall of Rome, specifically because of this moral prohibition against enslaving Catholics. When slavery did occur, it did so primarily in the easternmost parts of Europe, in Byzantium, and in the Muslim parts of Spain, and its primary target gives us the word itself: the Slavs.

The Slavs were excepted from the Catholic prohibition against slavery because they were not Catholic. Most had kept to their pagan ancestral ways or had converted to Eastern Orthodox Christianity. In either case, they were not part of the universal communion and therefore fair game for enslavement by Catholic kings and lords. This logic is how Europe later justified treating people in Africa just as they had treated the Slavs (*en-slav-ing* them, making them like the Slavs), because the people in Africa were not part of the universal communion.

Not all of Europe was Catholic by this point. Calvinism and Lutheranism had both arisen, as had the Anglican church a bit later. All three of these splinters from the universal communion, however, maintained the basic Catholic framework about slavery. It was sinful to treat other Christians as you would treat the Slavs, so if you wanted to enslave people, they needed to be non-Christians.

This has always been an important point that is extremely difficult for us moderns to grasp. The initial justifications for the transatlantic slave trade were not racial justifications. At that point in European history, there was no solidified concept of race, nor were people considered inferior based upon skin color. The concept of race developed in the early 17th century in response to a particular problem facing colonial administrators and religious leaders. Many of the Africans whom they had been treating as Slavs were converting to Christianity. So, too, were the conquered indigenous peoples. Suddenly, the religious prohibition against enslaving people who were part of the universal communion (and its variant Protestant forms) now also applied to the people who had been enslaved.

The crucial shift occurred in the American colonies during the very early part of the 1600s. Colonial administrators were facing social unrest due to the intermixing of lower-class European settlers (some of them indentured servants) with African slaves and indigenous population. The three groups had much more in common with each other than they did with the slave-owning colonial bosses.

Especially concerning for the colonial administrators was the cultural and religious intermixing. The European workers were adopting the religious beliefs and cultural norms of the people outside the communion, making it much more difficult for the authorities to control their behavior by insisting on religious conformity. At the same time, the Africans and indigenous people were syncretizing Christian ideas into their own religious practices, becoming nominally Christian.

This is how the concept of race was born. Colonial administrators began using the word "white" in laws and other legal documents to differentiate the lower-class Europeans from the other lower classes in the colonies. Negro (the Portuguese word for black) and other such terms soon became useful, legally. These words took on new meanings as well, referring not just to the apparent skin color of a person but to their place within the social order.

Return to Carl Schmitt's point again, which is that secular political forms are continuations of theological forms. You can probably already see that race is exactly this sort of continuation. In Catholic and later forms of Christianity, a set of protections and rights were to be universally applied, but only to those within that universe's theological bounds. Those within the catholic (remember: universal) communion were one sort of people, part of the same order of meaning (or theological order). Those outside that communion (outside the universal, a paradox I'd like you to consider for a moment) were a different sort of people completely, a kind of non-person to whom you could do anything, without divine repercussion.

Anathema

We've looked at the roots of race in Catholic theology, but we need to go even further back. The Catholics did not come up with this idea of universal communion on their own, but rather inherited and retooled a political-theological concept from the Roman Empire (the birthplace of Christianity), which inherited it from the Greeks. The Romans developed the idea of the *civitas*, which referred to everything to which the Roman order of meaning (its theological, political, cultural, and economic forms) could be applied. The *civitas* was the "universe," the place in which one (uni-) reality existed. Teasing out its etymology even further, the civitas was where everything had been turned (-verse) into one unified whole.

Of course, there was something outside the universe of the *civitas*. Rome was one universe, and outside that universe was the rest of the world, a place full of other ideas and peoples and beliefs over which Rome had no influence and against which Rome fought. That world outside the universe had multiple names, but one common Roman slur against the people who lived there was *paganus*. Originally a word meant to denote certain boundary markers at the edge of the *civitas*, *paganus* became synonymous with all those ideas, customs, beliefs, and ways of being in the world that had not thus far been conquered and subsumed into the universe.

The *civitas* was a continuation of the Greek concept of the *polis*, which specifically denoted the boundaries of the Greek city-states. Outside the *polis* was, again, the rest of the world, which for them was much larger and more of an object of curiosity than it was for the Romans. The Greek equivalent of universe is *kosmos*, a word that does not bear the same sense of unification as the Roman term.

For both the Greeks and the Romans, this outside realm, where their political and theological norms did not apply, held an element of terror and savagery. It was ultimately a land of monsters, of wolves, of strange languages and incomprehensible customs where the protections and benefits that came with being part of the Greek *polis* or the Roman *civitas* were not recognized.

One of the worst punishments that you could suffer in Greece or in Rome was to be expelled into that outside realm and never be allowed to return. The Roman version of this concept was called *homo sacer*, literally "sacred man." The person who was *homo sacer* was stripped of all the legal protections the Roman *civitas* granted and "given over to the gods." Another way of putting this now would be to say they were "thrown to the wolves," which were, for thousands of years in Europe, the symbol of all that lay outside the community.

The Greeks had a similar concept, that of *anathema*. A thing was anathema when it was taken out of the world and given over to the gods (by sacrifice), with a later connotation of being "expelled" or "banished" from the mundane, everyday world.

Anathema is better known, in its later Christian use, as a form of excommunication or as a descriptor of a thing that is so evil it must be banished or destroyed. Returning to the earlier conversation about the progression from universal communion to the modern concept of race, consider what excommunication actually was: Not just "we don't talk to that person any longer," (the current sense of the word) but rather complete ejection from the universe. A person who was excommunicated was "thrown to the wolves," their fate left up to the one-god.

When the Pope excommunicated a king, for example, all other Christian kings were free to wage war against him and his kingdom. An individual who was excommunicated could be killed on sight, or treated as the Slavs were treated, and no other person within the universal communion was permitted to give them help, aid, or protection.

Anathema was the original word used by the early Christian authorities for what later became excommunication. Anathema was later replaced by *excommunicatus*, probably for two reasons. First, since the core meaning of *anathema*, in Greek, was "to devote to the gods"—with the sense of banishment being only a secondary connotation—the word was a bit too extreme to fit all the many reasons a person might be expelled from the community. The more important reason, I suspect, is that anathema denotes a permanent state. When something is given over to the gods (or in the Christian order, the God), anyone taking it back (that is, allowing the person back into the universal communion) is committing a blasphemy.

So, anathema became the term used for the extreme excommunication of people based on unpardonable sins for which there existed no possibility of redemption and reconciliation. A person who was excommunicated could later be re-admitted to the universe by confessing their sins and showing penance, but a person who was anathema was so sinful, so in error, that they could never return.

Beliefs Beyond the Pale

What was so unforgivable that it would make a person anathema rather than *excommunicatus*?

Heresy.

Heretical beliefs did not only make you subject to becoming anathema, the beliefs were anathema themselves. To hold, to speak, and especially to teach heretical beliefs to others was a sin for which you could never be forgiven, nor could a heretic ever be re-admitted into the universal communion.

For the Catholic Church, some beliefs were so extreme that those who held them posed an existential threat to the very order of things. Questioning the trinity, the divinity of Jesus or his simultaneous dual nature, the existence of the Church as the one mediator between man and God (and the Pope as the vicar of Christ, Christ's stand-in on earth), or the virginity of Mary—subjected the questioner not just to excommunication but also to becoming anathema.

Other ideas were similarly *verboten*. Most of the millenarian sects were seen as anathema because they held beliefs which were seen as anathema. Some of those ideas appear to us now to be merely esoteric and theological—infant baptism or questioning the celibacy of the priesthood, for example—and we can reduce the response to them as apparent over-reaction or purposeless exercise of authority. This is a deeply short-sighted view, however, as it misses how such ideas were key aspects of the political order of the universal communion.

Take the issue of infant baptism. The act of christening a child literally made them Christian, which brought them into the universal communion. It conferred a kind of citizenship upon the person in the same way that the circumcision of boys in Judaism brings those boys into the covenant. Thus, to question the age at which children were baptized—or to suggest that some sort of confession or statement of faith should be made before a person is included into the universal communion—undermined the theoretical framework of the universal communion itself.

The second anathema idea that I mentioned—the celibacy of the priesthood—has a deeply political dimension that is often overlooked. The requirement that a priest (and remember they were all men) remain celibate meant that any children he might have would be illegitimate and thus have no property claims through their father. Therefore, church property and wealth would never be transferred out of the church to the children of the priests but would always remain the property of Rome.

The point to remember here is that anathema was a category reserved for heresies that threatened the very order of things, rather than for ideas that were merely deviant or false. Anathema challenged the foundations of society, of the universal communion, of civilization itself, and those who embraced ideas that were anathema needed to be expelled as far away from society as possible.

There is a phrase we use in English whose origins tend to be quite obscured: "beyond the pale." For an idea or an action to be beyond the pale, it must be so far removed from the norms of civil society that it cannot be countenanced at all, but must be fought and banished.

The root of this phrase comes from a particular boundary line drawn by the English in their conquest and occupation of Ireland. A "pale" is a boundary marker, literally a wooden stake placed into the ground (it is the root of the English word "pole") and comes from

Latin *palus*. The phrase itself was used in the 1500's to describe the uncivilized, unconquered, "savage" territory in Ireland where English law and customs had not taken hold. It was a place to be terrified of (especially if you were an English soldier) and, incidentally, a place a person could run to if they were excommunicated or otherwise exiled from civilization (as, say, bandits, whose name means ""those who were banished").

If the area "beyond the pale" sounds like the same conception as the Roman *paganus* (a *pagus* was a boundary marked by just this sort of *palus*), then you have already begun to understand my larger meaning. Consider again the way we use that phrase now. We do not use it to describe a physical place at all, but rather an extreme way of thinking or acting that is utterly unacceptable. In fact, we use it the same way that the Catholic Church used the word anathema, describing ideas that need to be forcefully expelled from everyday reality lest they cause untold damage or even undermine the order of meaning itself.

Crucial to excommunication, and especially to anathema, was that the punishment relied on other people enacting it. The person who was anathema had to be collectively punished, collectively banished from the universal community. Fellow villagers, family members, local lords, priests, and all those in surrounding areas were told of the person's anathema status, and each knew that the punishment for helping such a person was becoming anathema themselves. Ultimately, the person who was anathema was chased out of civilization (if they were not killed, an act for which the killer was immediately granted forgiveness).

They were pushed out past the boundaries, the borders, beyond the pale, into the wilderness, the lands of the pagans, and even further: out of the (localized) universal and into the world, the "bare life" of animals and trees, far from human help or companionship. Because they had offended the god(s), they were given over to the gods, who would be the final judges of the person's fate.

Of course, that world "beyond the pale" wasn't empty, nor were the vast lands outside the borders of the *civitas* or *polis*. A world existed outside of the universe, beyond the reach of the order of meaning the exiled person's anathema beliefs threatened to destroy. Beyond the pale were the Irish, who were hardly savage or uncultured. Outside the reach of Rome were myriad cultural groups with their own orders of meaning.

The crime and proclamation of anathema only had power within the order of meaning which that anathema threatened to destroy. If you could escape the reach of that order of meaning, you were free, no longer subject to its rules or proclamations. Most of all, you were free from the violent mob justice of the universal communion, the collective hatred the order of meaning had summoned to its defense against anathema.

We return once again to Carl Schmitt's point here: Our modern political forms are continued theological forms. Anathema continues to be an unforgivable crime for which there is no possible redemption, regardless of whether modern social media mobs understand the historical concept. Fortunately, as it turns out, there's a world outside the universe. In fact, countless worlds. We shouldn't be so afraid of venturing out into those worlds, nor should we understand banishment to them to be any real punishment at all.

"So What?"

Some people are afraid of being themselves. Many people allow their lives to be limited by that fear. They play a continual game, fashioning a careful persona that they think the world will accept or admire. Even when they are in their solitude, they remain afraid of meeting themselves. One of the most sacred duties of one's destiny is the duty to be yourself. When you come to accept yourself and like yourself, you learn not to be afraid of your own nature. At that moment, you come into rhythm with your soul, and then you are on your own ground. You are sure and poised. You are balanced. It is so futile to weary your life with the politics of fashioning a persona in order to meet the expectations of other people. Life is very short, and we have a special destiny waiting to unfold for us. Sometimes through our fear of being ourselves, we sidestep that destiny and end up hungry and impoverished in a famine of our own making.

John O'Donahue, Anam Cara

Coming out is an odd idea. I've never liked the phrase, even though the process it describes is a rather profound one. A gay guy "comes out" when he admits to himself and those around him that he desires men and not women, with the sense that he was previously hiding all of this. There's a metaphorical closet, as the saying goes, that some of us are stuck in until we decide to open the door and leave it.

The origin of the phrase is actually a mixed metaphor produced by the conflation of two different expressions. "Coming out" was the term, in the early part of last century, for the process in which a young woman was formally introduced to society through a series of parties. Those parties constituted her "début" into the social circles of her class standing, and the woman making her début was thus a "débutante."

As has often been the case, this feminine social ritual was adopted by American gay culture. A gay man's coming out was his début into the underground networks of gay society. There he would be introduced to other men, including those he may have already known in public life without knowing, until his début, that they were gay. In other words, it was a celebration and an initiation, and according to some accounts by historians of gay culture it was once a really serious affair.

Then there's a second part of the expression: the closet. The closet was added later by those who did not know the original context for coming out, and it referred not to something important and celebratory but rather to something negative, the dark secret some people are attempting to hide. The "skeleton in the closet," conflated with the feminine social ritual of coming out, became "coming out of the closet."

So already the expression is deeply clunky. I've never been much for the idea that a man desiring men must therefore emulate feminine rituals (or behavior, or speech patterns, etc.), since it's precisely my lack of desire for the feminine and my desire instead for the masculine that is at the root of what we call being gay. Why then try to copy ridiculously caricatured ideas of womanhood? On the other hand, the "skeleton" metaphor is a bit more useful. As an adolescent,

I sensed that there was something dark, evil, and malignant lingering in the recesses of my private thoughts, something I needed to hide from everyone around me. What if my male friends knew I found them attractive? What if my female friends found out I wasn't a "real" man? What if the church I attended discovered this dark secret, or others at school? I was certain they'd all judge me exactly the way I judged myself: as perverted, broken, and not worthy of ever being taken seriously.

My "coming out" was hard, but it was much less eventful than my paranoid fears had worked it up to be. I started telling a few close friends in the Christian college I went to that I thought I "maybe might be gay," and they all promised to pray for me so that I wouldn't be. I told my dad next, and he assured me that I wasn't really gay because he'd had lots of sexual experiences with other guys as a teenager and he'd ended up straight, regardless. I'd not really wanted to know that about him, and anyway I'd had no experiences at all, so that conversation wasn't very helpful although, to his credit, he wasn't mean about it.

What I'd thought would be the hardest confession experience was almost a letdown. I had a friend whom I respected intensely, someone I took to be my intellectual superior (and honestly, I'm still certain he's much more intelligent than I am). He was also a bit of an asshole, by which I mean he didn't really tolerate boring statements or anything that he saw as emotionally over-wrought. I was certain he'd berate me or, worse, completely ignore my existence once I told him. Yet I told him.

"So what?" he replied. It was not, at all, a question.

Despite the fact that my coming out was generally easy—meaning that it wasn't as terrifying as I'd fantasized—it was not without consequences. I still felt like I'd betrayed everyone, that I was somehow lesser than everyone else, and especially that I'd disappointed people I liked and respected. I lost my scholarship to the Christian college I attended because I was gay, took out exorbitant student loans, and still haven't paid off that debt nor did I ever finish college. I definitely lost some friends, including someone I considered to be my best friend, and the entire trajectory of my life changed.

That trajectory changed for the better, I should note, despite the fact that it may have messed up my life for a few years. There were years when I didn't know what the hell I was doing, or what I was supposed to do, or even what I was capable of doing. But I'm not certain that all wouldn't have happened anyway. I learned long ago that laying the blame for poverty and mental distress on "oppression" as a "minority identity" is really just an abdication of personal agency.

We imagine things are going to be much, much worse, when we resolve to act true to ourselves, than they ever really are. Which isn't to say that it can't still be awful. Because let's be honest: it's horrible to have people reject you, horrible to have people call you names or declare you morally corrupt. Worst of all may be realizing that some of the people you really liked and respected now think you're evil.

When you "come out" as a gay man, what you're really doing is leaving an entire order of respectability and meaning to which you were seen as belonging. Gay guys who do this later in life have it much, much harder than a teenager does, regardless of what the kids these days will tell you. I've known so many men who didn't decide to act according to their desires until their forties or fifties, and by that point they've got a lot more to account for than just wanting to feel the touch of another man. They're usually married with kids, having done lots of work to maintain the role they thought was expected of them.

The really horrible part is, by that point, those role expectations are justified. It's one thing to defy the expectation that a 16-year-old will one day get married and be a husband and father. But a guy who actually got married and actually had children is expected to be a husband and a father because he already is those things. Trying to re-negotiate all of that is always messy for everyone. Even then, however, though things will probably be horrible, they'll almost certainly be less horrible than the guy fears.

Writing what you think is true—even and especially if it's not what others expect you to write—works the same way. It's coming out of one social order and one order of meaning into another one, and it's like coming out as a gay man in another way, too. See, there's actually no cool début ritual for gay guys anymore, if there ever really was one. Instead, there's a lot of fumbling about in dark rooms without anyone to guide you or explain everything to you.

Sometimes it's utter hell. Not long after my coming out, I was drugged and raped by someone that everyone else told me was an amazing and really good person. They said those things again and more loudly after I told them what he'd done, and suddenly there were certain places I couldn't go anymore because people would harass me about falsely accusing him. People don't want to hear things that challenge their views, and they don't want to think that the people they respect are actually quite awful, so they'll call you whatever names fit best, in order to erase your words from their world.

That kind of thing is universal. You don't have to be gay or be a writer to experience an entire crowd of people rallying around someone they prefer over you. Humans do that, and they always think they are being "good" and doing the "right thing" by trying to silence the threat to their social order.

I've been called as many different names, as a writer, as I was called after coming out, and the experience is really no different. Oddly, though, I never heard gay slurs, back then, as often as I hear "fascist," or "racist," or "transphobe," now. That's where the analogy breaks down, because honestly it was a lot more pleasant to be a gay man around people who didn't like gays in America than it is to be a leftist writer who challenges social justice identitarianism.

That being said, it's the same social mechanism at play. Pierre Bourdieu's brilliant point about categorization is that it still preserves the original Greek meaning of "accuse" (*kategorein*), and in both senses it is an attempt to institute an order of meaning and division.

Calling a guy a "faggot" or a "girl" because he desires men is an attempt to assert that he is somehow less man than other men, instituting a division within the category of men between "real" men and "fake" men. Categorizing—that is, accusing—a man to be "effeminate" because he desires other men is the same attempt to institute division, asserting that there are men who act as men should and men who, instead, act as women should.

Unfortunately, accusations often stick and become internalized. Much of the reason why gay men adopted feminine cultural rituals like the "coming out" début, call each other "girl" and "queen," and accuse gay men who don't adopt these affectations of having "internalized homophobia" is precisely because they were accused of (categorized as) really being women themselves.

This is the core problem of all modern identity politics, of course. *Kategorein* is used to create and shape an identity. You are told that you are a different kind of human because you are black or homosexual or disabled; you believe it and then shape your identity according to that accusation. Of course, shaping yourself according to others' perceptions only reinforces the instituted division, eventually manifesting their accusation as true.

Earlier I mentioned the friend who said, "So what?" when I came out to him. That was at least 25 years ago now, and it took almost as long to understand that, in his apparently callous indifference to my internal struggles, he'd given me a profound gift. Others who knew me at that time can attest to the really clumsy and ridiculous affectations I attempted after my coming out. I tried to "act" gay, bought "gay" clothes, raised my voice into a higher register than my natural one, and started listening to Madonna on repeat.

"What the fuck are you doing?" he said to me. Again, not a question.

Full of self-righteousness, I answered angrily, "I'm gay—you have a problem with that?"

"You think you have to act like that to be gay?"

I didn't answer, but I immediately stopped. It had all felt so deeply fake anyway. I hated the clothes, I hated trying to change my voice, and honestly, I really hated Madonna. Of course, no one had actually told me I needed to change the way I acted or what I consumed to be gay: instead, I'd constructed this identity from all the accusations and caricatures I'd heard about gay guys and tried to emulate it.

In other words, I'd believed the accusation, accepted the category, and tried to fit into what I thought was expected of me.

It's easier to do that, at least initially. Borrowing meaning from others saves you the work of finding your own meaning, but it also guarantees that you'll postpone an inevitable and difficult process to a later time when it'll be much more difficult. As with the married father in his forties trying to renegotiate all of his commitments and obligations so that he can finally be true to himself, it just gets much messier the later you leave it.

John O'Donohue, the Irish Hegelian mystic and poet, wrote that the work of the soul gets harder the longer we put it off; the longer we avoid it, the more we "end up hungry and impoverished in a famine of our own making." The earlier you learn to like yourself, to enjoy your own company, and to discover who it is you really are outside of (and despite of) what others think of you, the richer, the more meaningful, and the happier your life will be.

Categories and accusations are never meaningful unless you let them be. Letting others define who you are is a deep betrayal of your own soul and your own agency in the world. Letting others define you by defining yourself against their expectations, trying to prove otherwise, is just as much a betrayal, and is the most inauthentic thing a person could ever do.

So, I write. I write as I see things because I write from who I am, not who I think I should be, nor who others want me to be. It's the work of the soul, which is its own reward. Thanks to all of you, it's also meant that, for the first time in my life, I earn enough money from writing to live well. It's probably no mere coincidence that being more myself resulted in attracting so much material support from others, but even if it hadn't, I'd do it all anyway. The work of the soul is what Nietzsche meant when he said, "Become who you are."

That's what I'd tell any writer who is holding back their own words out of fear: Become who you are. And if others accuse you for it, don't let that matter. Say, as a friend once said to me, "So what?"

And never mean it as a question.

The Mirror in the Abyss

The most radical of my former friends, the ones most devoted to changing the world and shaking from the thrones of the earth all the false gods that oppress them, have always also been the most unhappy.

Someone who knew me well, more than a decade and a half ago, had a rather interesting way of describing my politics back then. We were at a party, and someone was talking admiringly about my political work and extensive knowledge of anarchist and critical theory. He smiled approvingly, and then said, "Yeah, and his politics are indistinguishable from his coping mechanisms."

He hadn't meant it as an insult, and I hadn't taken it that way either. In fact, the person with whom we spoke agreed that such a way of going about politics was probably the most integrated thing one might do. After all, "the personal is political," and therefore the political is personal, and why shouldn't they constantly inform each other?

The answer is that, for me, that enmeshment was quite personally destructive, although it took me until just a few years ago to see this. To recount everything that this way of being entailed would take an entire book, one that perhaps I'll write someday. To trace precisely where it started would also take more words than I have time to write.

The best place to begin may be at the end, the moment I finally understood that I had been sabotaging myself for decades.

That was almost four years ago now. I was dodging thrown books and a hurled laptop while trying to step, barefoot, over broken glass. It was 4 AM on a rainy December morning. I was desperately tired, and terrified, and also wondering how I'd gotten myself into this position... again.

What happened was that the physically and mentally abusive man I'd been with for the previous year and a half was having another psychotic break. He'd stopped taking his medications (primarily ones for sleep) because they were "oppressing" him, and since I was "causing" his current anxiety he was attacking me. This wasn't the first time. He'd kicked me before, and punched me several times, and one night he woke me up by dumping a very large amount of dirt on me while I slept. There were many other such incidents, but I think you probably already understand that it was generally quite awful.

As I said, this wasn't the first time I'd been in such a position. He wasn't the first lover to attack me. Another, six years earlier, smashed everything in the room we shared, pulling down all the drywall from the walls and punching out the windows as well as a very large mirror. I'd had nowhere else to sleep that night, so after he left I swept as much of the broken glass and drywall off of the bed as I could, wrapped myself in a blanket, and cried myself to sleep.

Those two were not my only bad relationships. A third was with a man addicted to crystal meth. Something that he did to me, despite my protests (I'll spare you the details), meant that I couldn't have receptive sexual relations for almost two years afterward.

When something like that happens once to you, it's awful. When it happens multiple times, it's a pattern. That final relationship was the perfect storm of all my shitty beliefs about myself. While that guy was extremely awful, I couldn't deny that this time I'd actually walked right into the situation and closed the cage door behind me. That's what I told the therapist I started working with after the last incident. I fled from France to my sister's home in Luxembourg to get away from him, and after ten days of staring into the abyss that had become my life, that abyss became a mirror. Every single stupid belief about the world, that had guided me into such traps, stared back at me. I finally understood that I was an unwitting but nevertheless active agent in my own suffering.

That therapist was damn good, by the way. Like all good ones, he was adept at creating a space in which you constantly answer your own questions and become really impatient with all the ridiculous ideas to which you've too long clung.

I believed I took up too much space in the world because I was different from others. I believed that the "real" me was too much for other people. Others who seemed to be able to act authentically, or to move about the world without feeling the need to apologize for themselves, were either people without real depth or they were indifferent to the needs of others.

I believed there is never enough for everyone, and so it's best to wait until everyone else has what they need first. This belief was clearly rooted in my childhood poverty, when there literally was not enough to eat (sometimes there was just toast with margarine for dinner). This later manifested in the belief that my own needs, problems, and desires needed to be postponed until everyone else's were met. And while this all sounds noble, the result of this way of thinking is always deep resentment at others who don't do the same thing.

I believed I could only react to miserable conditions, rather than create better conditions for myself. Again, this obviously came from my childhood when I was literally unable to create better conditions for myself. It took me more than 20 years of adulthood to stop acting like I was still a defenseless child, and especially to let go of the sense that others were responsible for making things better.

And I believed that suffering was always a symptom of injustice and always had an external cause. Here's where the particular form of political ideology I embraced became indistinguishable from my coping mechanisms: When bad things happened to me, I was powerless to do anything about it until some great other (a system, an employer, an imagined oppressor) was held to account.

This last belief deserves a lot more attention, as it's become a core feature in political ideology.

Consider how the accusation of "victim blaming" denies the agency of the victim. If anyone even cautiously dared point out to me that I seemed to have a pattern of getting into abusive relationships, and also a pattern of staying in such relationships long past the point when I understood that they were not good for me, I could easily have called those observations "victim blaming."

It is fully true that others were acting abusively to me. I was not asking for the abuse nor causing them to be abusive. But that's not the entire story. I realized that I kept getting myself into such situations. While I was not the cause of the abuse, I was absolutely responsible—and I was the only one with that agency—for the decision to enter into those relationships and to stay in them. Sure, there were practical, material concerns involved (immigration status, housing insecurity, etc.), but looking back now I understand that my view of the options available to me was also self-limited.

The political problem here—which is also a social, cultural, and spiritual problem—is that we have stifled our ability to talk about personal agency in favor of a cult of victimhood and an esoteric belief in structural injustice. We see causation occurring in only one direction, and seethe with righteous fury when anyone dares suggest that a person might be able to affect their own circumstances.

Worse, we then encourage those in such situations (ourselves and others) to see victimhood as virtuous. This is what Nietzsche meant by the "slave morality" and *ressentiment*, a psychological shift in which we try to compensate for or cope with a feeling of injustice by convincing ourselves that suffering is sacred and morally good. As part of the current social media trend to elevate behavioral and mental disorders and disabilities (ADHD, for example, and even schizophrenia, as well as the more extreme ends of the "fat-positivity" movement) to cool or unique personal traits, or in the ritualistic celebration of oppression identities, we raise shrines and temples to, and create idols of, suffering itself. Victims become the chosen ones, the elect, the favored of the divine, and it is almost embarrassing to admit that you have not suffered as others have.

Those were once my own politics, which were also my coping mechanisms. I didn't want to be poor. I didn't want to be in abusive relationships. I didn't want to suffer so constantly from depression or from the consequences of my ridiculous beliefs about the world. Adopting a political framework that told me none of it was my fault was the worst thing I could possibly have done for myself. It was worse than all the abuse, worse than all the poverty, worse than all the suffering. Nevertheless, it felt better than actually looking into the abyss.

When I finally got out of that last situation and started unraveling those beliefs, I lost lots of friends, and fast. What is clear to me now (though it never was before) is that I had actively pushed away those who could help me out of these messes, and instead sought out other broken and miserable people as full of *ressentiment* as I was. It was easy for us all to find each other, of course, because we styled ourselves activists and dropped hints in our speech with cues like "intersectionality" and "structural injustice."

I somehow managed to keep a few authentic friends throughout those years. The rest of them—all with happy lives and stable relationships and an outlook on life that didn't involve blaming everyone else for their own problems—had wisely given up trying to be my friend, They'd departed because they had good boundaries, and cared enough about their own happiness and health to cut a destructive element out of their lives, even if that element was someone they liked.

Their withdrawal was a gift and a kindness, because when I finally looked into the abyss, I realized I needed to do the same kind thing for myself.

So here I am now, a few years after I finally decided to stop all this idiocy. You don't undo decades of self-destructive thinking immediately. There are times that I still catch myself blaming some external force or person for situations that I willingly got myself into. Occasionally I look at the successes of others and tell myself that I cannot have the same success, that I am somehow different from them. Sometimes I still fear taking up space in the world and hesitate before asking for what I want and need. And sometimes I'll let a miserable situation continue rather than applying the (often very slight) effort required to change it.

I'm happily married now, and to a man who has no patience for *ressentiment.* He once told me that I should either stop acting like I cannot become what I want to be, or I should consider our relationship over. That may sound harsh, perhaps, but it's exactly what I needed to hear. The friends I've made since then have no tolerance for my former ways of thinking either, and they're much kinder and much more fun to be around than any of those I had to jettison a few years ago.

I imagine that the stability, joy, wealth, and deep feeling of agency I have now would all be labeled as "privilege" by those former friends. And though I know they'll write it off as "victim blaming" when I say this, I'll say it anyway:

You don't have to be miserable, and you have much more agency over your own life than your wrong beliefs about yourself and the world allow you to see. There is no virtue in suffering, and it is cruel to yourself and others to pretend otherwise. Your politics should never be your coping mechanism, and your coping mechanisms should never be your politics. Also, seriously: Don't ever let someone abuse you a second time. The first time is fully on them, but the second time is also on you. Get out of there, no matter the cost.

Polytheistic Pluralism and Sacred Cows

I'm a polytheist, which means that I recognize the existence of multiple gods rather than just one or none. That may sound like an unusual or ridiculous thing to believe, but I'm hardly alone. About 1.35 billion people are at least nominal adherents to Hinduism, a figure which, alone, should point to the less-than-unusual nature of my belief.

Whether you agree with my position or not does not concern me. Most people I encounter don't, and that's perfectly fine. As a matter of fact, a core feature of polytheism is its complete lack of interest in proselytizing or gatekeeping. Unlike monotheistic religions which have initiatory rituals (circumcision, baptism) to help decide who is in and who is out, what makes you an adherent to a polytheistic religion is simply your acceptance of that particular cosmology.

This core difference derives from a more profound difference in the ways that polytheists and monotheists see the world and understand divinity. For a polytheist, the world is inhabited by many centers of meaning and value, none of which truly supplant or undermine the other. Order therefore arises from difference and chaos organically, the way that people with completely different backgrounds and histories and ideas can find themselves becoming friends.

"Polytheistic" Pluralism

For a polytheist, the world is a lot more like a forest than a garden. Polytheism results in a kind of pluralism that can be a bit maddening for some, and potentially even seem post-modern or agnostic because of its willingness to accept the "truths" of others without necessarily buying into their universals.

Consider, for example, how most people of good will are likely to react when someone tells them they have seen a ghost. Generally, such an account is a matter of interest but not a matter of judgment. We're willing to accept that the other person experienced something they call a ghost without necessarily deciding that ghosts must therefore exist. Something was experienced, and the person who experienced it called it a ghost, and that's all that (usually) matters.

In fact, I suspect this kind of pluralism is the default state for most people who are not otherwise captured by ideology. Consider the most common reaction I've heard from people, in person, regarding the matter of trans identity. Most are happy to accept that someone considers their gender to be different from their biological sex, and to make efforts to use the pronouns a person requests. In this kind of pluralism, what doesn't necessarily follow from such interactions is a simultaneous change in their personal beliefs about what a man or a woman is—because it doesn't need to. Just like we don't need to change our own cosmology because someone we know says they saw a ghost. We can accept their experience of things, and also our own, without conflict, and then go about the business of actually living life alongside each other.

The monotheistic framework—and its modern offshoots, including secular liberalism and even atheism—deals in universals. Universals are not necessarily a bad thing, because ideas like "universal human rights" are products of this way of thinking. So too, unfortunately, are a lot of our ideas about identity, government, and the nation-state.

To understand how this works in the sphere of personal relations, consider again the matter of ghosts. If a person claims they saw a ghost, the monotheistic framework then poses a binary question: "Are there ghosts, or are there not?" If the listener believes in ghosts, there is no conflict. If the listener doesn't believe in ghosts, however, they are likely to dismiss the claim of the speaker. And if the speaker insists and is persuasive, or if the listener has a lot of reason to otherwise trust the speaker, then a crisis of belief will arise. Consider again the matter of trans identity. Within a pluralistic/polytheistic framework one is content to accept someone's professed identity without necessarily changing one's own conceptions. The monotheistic framework asks, "Is this person really a woman (or man)?"

A lot of the conflict—on both sides—around trans identity comes down to the need for universality within a monotheistic framework. So, people who insist that "no matter how you feel, you are actually this instead" are approaching the question from within a monotheistic framework. And those who insist that it isn't enough merely to accept someone's preferred identity without also changing one's own beliefs about what constitutes a man or a woman are using the monotheistic framework as well.

To put this in simpler terms, polytheistic pluralism allows for multiple realities that don't necessarily cancel each other out, even if they are in conflict. I might have completely different beliefs about something than someone else, and that just makes life more interesting and rich. It's when we insist that there is only one true belief about a thing that we come into conflict.

By now you've probably noticed that "polytheist" and "monotheist" don't precisely map to particular religious affiliations. There are plenty of Christians and Muslims who approach the world from within a much more pluralistic framework than the doctrines of their religions would like them to. This is because pluralism is really the human default, when ideology doesn't take hold of us. Most of us are usually pretty happy to just get along with people regardless of our differing opinions about the world. Opinions don't really constitute the majority of our in-person social interactions. You're not usually verifying your bus driver's opinions about capitalism or Black Lives Matter before taking her bus or checking to make sure your grocery clerk shares your ideas about abortion or Brexit before you let him ring up your order.

We generally prefer to just live alongside each other without ideological conflict, unless there is some external pressure exacerbating those ideological differences.

Either-or? Or and-also?

This was the subject of my first presentation at a polytheist conference 2014. I'm sure I wrote it out less succinctly than I have here, and I know my hands were shaking fiercely as I read from a print-out of my speech, but it went very well. The next year I volunteered to co-organize a conference outside of Seattle, where I lived at the time. That was a lot of work, but the result was even better than I had hoped. We had several hundred people attend, and presentations I heard at that conference still shape the way I think now.

I should probably disclose something else at this point: I was a bit of a hotheaded American leftist back then. I'm still a leftist and still a polytheist, but fortunately a lot less hotheaded.

Gods&Radicals Press, the publishing organization I run and co-founded, started around the time of that second conference. As the name implies, it was about polytheism and leftism, though of course we were also okay with people who weren't deeply identified with more than one of those threads. We also happily published writing from Christians, Sikhs, Jews, Atheists, and Muslims.

All this was happening right about the time political stuff in the United States was heating up. Worrying about the "alt-right" had become a media trend, and Antifa actions had begun against specific figures in that movement. I got caught up in all of that, as did other polytheists and, I think, members of every other sub-cultural movement in the United States.

I was on the "good" side, meaning Antifa. This is not how I look at it now, but at the time I was pretty damn certain that one side was completely right, and one side was completely wrong, and I wasn't going to be on the wrong side. But that's where I was wrong. Looking back, I realize that there wasn't a right side and a wrong side at all, just two opposing ideological positions rising out of the same monotheistic universalism I'd been arguing against at conferences and in speeches. If I had to choose between those two positions again, I'd probably make the same choice. As much as that early opposition to the alt-right has now morphed into a neoliberal juggernaut pushing people into *ressentiment* and totalitarian thinking, the other side was just plain idiotic and mean.

But those weren't the only possible choices, and it's taken me years to understand the damage I caused, and what I became by refusing to look for other options. I accumulated lots of social capital, sure, but the polytheist movement I had been so eager to build still hasn't recovered from what I did. What I did, by the way, was basically repeat the same formula, from George W. Bush, that extreme movements in the United States also repeat: "You're either with us, or you're with the terrorists." You can replace "terrorist," in that equation, with any word you like. No matter what, you always end up with the same monotheistic insistence on universalism. There are ghosts or there aren't, and there's absolutely no other way of approaching the matter.

Dr. Edward Butler and the Matter of Indica

I write all this as background for another story however, a story about what happened to a man I met at that first conference. He was a goofy-looking man, a professor with obvious professor glasses, and he asked me a question that was the absolute best compliment I'd ever received.

"Where did you go to grad school?" he asked.

I sheepishly admitted never even finishing college because of poverty and, rather than walking away in disgust, he smiled and said, "That's a shame. You write better than most academics I know."

His name is Dr. Edward Butler. He got in lots of trouble from some people for starting a polytheist initiative with an organization known as Indica. Indica is an academic and cultural organization promoting "global study of indigenous knowledge, seeking to bring about a renaissance of indigenous wisdom." As the name implies, Indica is based in India.

The problem, from the perspective of Edward Butler's accusers, is that some writers and academics with Indica lean heavily towards the Hindu identity movement known as *hindutva*. It's often seen as nationalist and has been primarily championed by the conservative ruling party in India, the Bharatiya Janata Party (BJP).

To get into all the nuances of this problem would take an entire book, but a few things can be cleared up quickly. Indica isn't part of the BJP or the nationalist youth movement, the RSS. Indica uses the term *hindutva* in a much broader and less political way than the BJP does, approximating the way "blackness" is used in the United States as a cultural identity formation. Indica's commitment to "dialogue across civilizations" and focus on Indic religions (including Buddhism, Jainism, and Sikhism) rather than Hinduism alone easily demonstrate that the accusations that Indica is really a Hindu-superiority outfit are false.

That being said, there's reason to be a little worried given the current situation in India. There are indeed many violent attacks against Muslims by Hindu nationalists, just as there have been many violent attacks on Hindus by Muslim extremists. There have also been very violent attacks on both groups by the secular Maoist Naxalites, much of whose funding comes from extortion and opiate production and trade.

Likewise, India is still suffering severely because of both its history of being a British colony and the centrist Indian National Congress party's disastrous neoliberal policies. Just as in Brazil and the United States, the legacy of this kind of globalized capital has been community destruction and labor crisis, creating fertile ground for right-wing populism. Though Narendra Modi, Jair Bolsonaro, and Donald Trump are very different people, they hold similar positions as figureheads of populist movements.

What distinguishes Modi and the BJP from the others, however, is the colonial history of India. India has only been independent from the British for about 70 years, and with British rule came a kind of enforced identity. Under colonial administration, religious affiliation became an identity category—something to be marked on official documents—rather than a profession or tribal affiliation. Colonialism required that, for the first time in thousands of years of their civilization's history, the people who lived in those lands had to define themselves by what they believed.

As I mentioned, polytheistic religions don't really do this. There is no initiatory or cultural gatekeeping regulating who is in or who is out, nor is there even a sense of either/or when it comes to religions. Yet, their colonial masters required that they suddenly define who they were in opposition to who others were.

Here's a good description of the problem the British caused, from a think tank otherwise critical of *hinduvta*:

> The need to distinguish the Indic religions from other religions in India lies in the impact made by the introduction of the Western term religion in the census operations carried out by the British in India, especially from 1871 onward. In these decennial or decadal censuses, the participants were asked to indicate their religious affiliation largely on the British assumption that one could only belong to one religion at a time. Some Indians began to feel over the years that this was having the effect of compartmentalizing what we might call the Indic religious tradition into four separate "religions." The key fact to keep in mind here is that the Indian followers of these four members of the Indic religious tradition did not treat their own relationship to these traditions necessarily in exclusive terms prior to the British intervention. In the Western conception of religion, a Jew, a Christian, and a Muslim had to be considered members of different religions (despite the fact that they worship one and the same God), whereas in the Indian conception of religious life, one could be a member of more than one tradition at the same time. Modern Nepalese, for instance, freely describe themselves as both Hindu and Buddhist, as they lay outside British jurisdiction.

So, it was the Christian British who imposed a kind of monotheistic thinking about religion onto the population of India. Monotheism tends towards exclusion, because it posits that there is only one god. On the other hand, polytheism has a peculiar and sometimes amusingly additive feature, resulting in the frustration of Christian missionaries when the indigenous peoples they tried to convert simply added Jesus to their own pantheon of gods and spirits.

From this colonial mess, then, arose the problem of identity in India, a problem that *hindutva* attempts to resolve. *Hindutva* poses the question, "What does it mean to be a Hindu?" in order to answer a question imposed upon them by the British: "Are you a Hindu?"

The answers to those questions have often been catastrophic and full of dead ends, especially in the hands of nationalist political movements. Any American reading this, however, needs to be aware that what seems like an obvious political parallel to the situation in the United States isn't a parallel at all. Though adherents to Indic religions (Buddhism, Jainism, Hinduism, and Sikhism) have been the majority in the territory of India, until 70 years ago they were also the oppressed, colonized peoples, ruled over by British authority.

The early nationalist movements in India were formed under colonial rule. They were national independence movements, and there were many of them. Some (including the movements eventually acknowledged by the British) were liberal secularist movements, while others articulated their anti-colonialism based on cultural and religious identity (drawing a distinction between their colonial masters and the people who were being oppressed by them).

Thus, the inclination of many to compare *hindutva* to American white nationalism is completely wrong. Instead, imagine if the First Nations in North America had managed to throw off colonial rule and then had to wrestle with the question, "What makes us native?" while trying to also figure out what to do with all the descendants of African slaves who were neither native nor part of the colonial regime but nevertheless wanted the same rights to land as indigenous people.

We can look to the former Palestinian Protectorate (now Israel/Palestine), or the Congo, or South Africa, or even Venezuela to see that post-colonial states don't have an easy road to peace and national integration.

Sacred Cows

India is in the same position, and *hindutva* is one of the proposed answers. It's caused quite a bloody mess, but organizations like Indica have attempted to make it more pluralistic. The problem is that the political situation in India is really awful, and suffering from the same sort of ideological abandonment that we see in the United States left.

Take, for example, the issue of cows. Everyone knows that cows are sacred to Hindus, right? Yet India also happens to be one of the largest exporters of beef in the world. How did that happen? Capitalism, of course.

But it's still more complicated. See, leftists in India (including Marxists), as well as more mainstream liberals, fiercely oppose any bans on the slaughter of cows. Their reasons are varied: Some think beef is necessary to keep the poor alive (despite so much of the beef being exported rather than eaten domestically), while others argue that sacred prohibitions on cow slaughter are reactionary and even fascist. In all cases though, they articulate their opposition to bans on cattle slaughter as a secularist issue, as a matter of "separation of church and state."

Remember, the cow is a sacred animal to Hindus. So here we come to the complicated problem: The only major political party to argue that cows are sacred and campaign on a promise to end cattle slaughter was the right-wing/conservative BJP. And they did so by evoking *hindutva*.

The BJP aren't the only ones who believe the slaughter should be stopped, but they are the only major political party to have made this part of their platform. There is some leftist support for such a ban, but many such leftists have been smeared as reactionary or fascist because of it. One such person is probably the most renowned intellectual of the anti-globalization movement, Vandana Shiva, whose work with peasant Dalit (the "untouchable" caste) women to protect traditional seed knowledge has made her an enemy of many multinational corporations. Shiva herself does not appear to subscribe to *hindutva* and has repeatedly written against identity-based violence (committed by both Muslims and Hindus), but none of that matters to her critics who see anything associated with traditional Indic knowledge, medicine, or belief as essentially fascist.

This is the exact same problem we see in the United States now, where even people with clearly professed leftist beliefs and antifascist stances are seen as fascist when any of their ideas intersect with anything the "bad people" also believe. This is what's happened to Dr. Edward Butler. Because he works with an organization that stands for things that overlap with right-wing iterations of *hindutva* (again, Indica is attempting to de-politicize *hindutva*,) Edward Butler, in the words of one critic, "might prove to be a danger to the Pagan community, and since hindutva is a form of fascism, that can't be tolerated." Other critics were even more alarmist in their assessments, suggesting—completely without evidence—that Butler is himself a fascist. In one of the most telling attacks, a writer compares all attempts that Butler has made to explain himself as the equivalent of a conservative in the United States whining that "not everyone who voted for Trump was a racist."

Here is the crux of the matter: The particular brand of American ideological certainty that we variously call "woke" or "social justice," which is ultimately a continuation of George W. Bush's infamous equation, is being applied internationally.

Edward Butler is no fascist, and Indica is not a fascist project. I suspect *hindutva* will lead to the same ideological dead-end that every other identity politics (blackness, whiteness, etc.) leads to, but there is nothing inherently fascistic about it. In the hands of right-wing political parties, *hinduvta* can do an immense amount of damage. However, if enough people attempt to steer it away from an imposed monotheistic framework ("Who is Hindu and who is not?") into a pluralistic framework (which is the mission of Indica, especially in their focus beyond Hinduism on all Indic religions), then *hinduvta* has the potential to be quite liberating.

Leftist Ideological Abandonment

At global issue is the question of religious belief and cultural identity, and how they play out within neoliberalism. In India, Hindu religious belief is an obstacle to the expansion of capitalist markets. However, since the Muslim and Christian minorities have no religious problems with cattle slaughter and beef consumption, neoliberal politicians and capitalist interests manipulate them against the Hindu majority.

There is an interesting parallel in Europe, where some nations have tried to institute (or have succeeded in instituting) bans on kosher and halal butchery of cattle in the name of "animal welfare." If those governments were actually interested in animal welfare, they could ban all cattle slaughter, or at least massively reform the industrial mass production of beef. But that's not the point. Kosher and halal butchery strictures (which are both religious and cultural) are a barrier to capitalist expansion of beef production, and must be undermined. Muslims and Jews who protested these bans were smeared as "religious extremists" in Europe, just as Hindus protesting cattle slaughter in India earned the same title.

A crucial point in the longer conversation about the current state of the left and the problem with ideological formations is this: In Europe, just as in India, the left parties are generally in support of the government policies. Thus, populist movements with "right-wing" features arise as the only political forces which speak to these interests. The problem is made worse by the reactive nature of leftists once these populist movements arise. In the United States, there was a genuine opportunity for populist opposition to neoliberal policies to become a broad-based leftist movement. Both Donald Trump and Bernie Sanders spoke strongly against the neoliberal policies that had led to stagnant wages, massive job losses, and increasing debt—all populist concerns. Unfortunately, by those concerned as deplorable, reactionary, or racist, their concerns were ceded to the right and Trump won in 2016.

I have long argued—as have many other leftists who reject social justice identity politics—that the only way to stop right-wing populist movements is to stop abandoning ideological territory to them. As Marx and Engles noted, the primary result of capitalist expansion is the destabilization of cultural traditions and societal relations:

> The bourgeoisie cannot exist without constantly revolutionising the instruments of production, and thereby the relations of production, and with them the whole relations of society. Conservation of the old modes of production in unaltered form, was, on the contrary, the first condition of existence for all earlier industrial classes. Constant revolutionising of production, uninterrupted disturbance of all social conditions, everlasting uncertainty and agitation distinguish the bourgeois epoch from all earlier ones. All fixed, fast-frozen relations, with their train of ancient and venerable prejudices and opinions, are swept away, all new-formed ones become antiquated before they can ossify. All that is solid melts into air, all that is sacred is profaned, and man is at last compelled to face with sober senses his real conditions of life, and his relations with his kind.

Populist movements are reactions to this destabilization, and right-wing political parties are quite adept at steering these reactions toward their own ends. Leftists, on the other hand, became even more reactive and make no distinction between the rightist political manipulation of the concerns of the people and the concerns themselves. What Indica has been attempting to do by expanding and de-politicizing *hinduvta* has potential beyond India. Dr. Edward Butler's work to expand dialogue about polytheism across the world likewise has great potential, or at least it did before he was accused of being fascist for doing that work.

Years ago, I made the very same mistake as Dr. Butler's accusers. I failed to notice that I was trapped in a monotheistic framework, forcing myself to answer a question whose only answers were binary. I was an idiot back then. I caused some harm and derailed something that is only now getting back on track. Unfortunately, it looks like it's pretty eager to go off the rails again, and I'm not very hopeful they won't make the same mistakes I did.

We need to stop doing this. We need to stop giving ground to right-wing movements and abandoning sites of potential transformation. The world cannot be neatly divided between "fascist" and "antifascist," or even between "right" and "left," any more than it can be neatly divided between "Western" and "Eastern," "Christian" and "Hindu," or "white" and "black." These are all rigid and fragile categories that we've created through a monotheistic framework of thinking, forcing universals where they cannot be applied.

The alternative to this is pluralism. I call this alternative polytheistic, but it isn't exclusive to polytheist religions. And I deeply believe it's our default state, the organic and natural way we tend to relate to each other when external ideologies are not setting the coordinates of meaning for us.

Many gods, one god, no god—these are only oppositional categories if we insist that they must be so. As Vandana Shiva noted in one of her essays, Muslims and Hindus together resisted colonial rule because of their shared desire to be free from authoritarian control. That rule was capitalist and modernizing, and it has reproduced itself in the neoliberal policies of both the Congress party and the BJP ever since independence. Their solidarity was like that of the early American colonies: African slaves, poor European workers, and colonized indigenous peoples intermixing and fighting together against colonial rule.

We need that kind of pluralistic solidarity again, and the only way to get there is to stop responding to Empire's demands that we define ourselves—and each other—through either/or categories.

The Secret of Crossings

The world outside my window is covered in a fine, gently falling mist as I write this. The water drips off the leaves of young willow and birch lining the banks of a stream that usually meanders but is now swollen by days of heavy rain.

That stream, which starts not far from my home, is called the Roudemerbaach, named for the reddish tint given to the water by the iron-rich clay of this land. We live in a high valley between two ridges of hills, the other sides of which descend much more steeply than ours does. So, the Roudemerbaach, along with its sister the Faaschtbaach (my favorite stream here, the "fasting" creek) which starts at the foot of an ancient sacred oak, are both gentle streams.

The two meet just below the place where the "last wolf" on this land was killed in the late 1800s. Soon after the streams meet they join the Syre, then meet the Sûre, then eventually join the Moselle and finally the Rhine, before flowing out to sea. On the other side of the hills, the White Ernz joins the Black Ernz, along with the Alzette (which runs through the center of Luxembourg city and is the cause of the massive gorge cutting through it) and all three meet the Sûre downstream from where the creek outside my window does.

All these streams flooded last night.

Last night, just as we started cooking dinner, we got a panicked call from my partner's best friend. The police in her town were warning everyone that the river would flood its banks in a particularly dangerous way, a "100-year flood." She and her family live along the bank on the German side of the Sûre (on their side it is called the Sauer). Their village is just upstream from my stream's eventual meeting with the river, but just downstream from where the streams starting on the other side of this hill meet it.

Another river on the German side, the Prüm, joins the Sauer just a few kilometers upstream from their village, putting them just below the confluence of three flooding rivers.

We quickly changed into work clothes, and my partner drove us to their home. The rain was intense, and quite a few fallen trees blocked the streets, causing us to reroute several times. The primary bridge across the Sauer was flooded, so we needed to detour upriver yet again before crossing.

Because I was not driving, I watched with awe the world of water that the land had become. It may seem morbid, but I love "natural disasters." By which I mean not the destruction they cause but the raw and profound natural forces that they are. Disasters are horrible. But the floods, forest fires, heatwaves, earthquakes, volcanic eruptions, and all the natural things that cause them, were once seen as manifestations of gods, or as gods themselves. When we humans looked above us into the night sky to find meaning, rather than into the glowing screens in our hands, we saw the stars as connected to the events of our lives. A disaster was a *dis-astra*—a "bad" or "ill" star—a moment when our connection to those lights so incomprehensibly far away was somehow sundered (the pre-Latin root of dis-).

I watched as the rivers rose around us, staring in particular awe at the force of the Prüm as we crossed it. Just before it joined the Sauer, its waters seemed to jump straight upward as if they came from deep within the earth itself. It was both beautiful and terrifying to watch, and it boded poorly for the fate of our friend's village, but nevertheless, seeing such power, three words escaped my lips:

"Hail to you," I said.

I don't know when I started doing this, but it's been years now. I greet the moon, or particularly ancient trees, or an intensely warm sun, or a lightning storm or strong wind this way. I say this to animals of particular presence, as I do when there are wild boars about, or on the night I heard a wolf howl on a nearby hill. I greet most ravens this way, especially when they assemble and conspire in the branches of the ancient oak outside our home.

"Hail" is the old Nordic/Germanic word for "health" and "fortune," and is also the root of the English word "holy" via the German *heilige*. "Health" shares the same root as well. Thus, something that was holy was healthy, "whole" and "intact," and thus full of fortune. Saying "hail" to someone wishes them those virtues, or acknowledges those virtues in them which, to the animist mind, is the exact same thing.

These massive and uncontrollable forces are beautiful to me. They fill me with awe and a strange sense of delight. Not because of the destruction they cause but in reverent response to their very existence as forces pure and true and fully outside our human world.

We crossed the Prüm and arrived in the village to which we had sped. Our friend's house is quite old. I imagine it is a beautiful place in less chaotic circumstances. We arrived just as others did; her cousin, another friend, two neighbors. She hugged us, and though I do not know her well it was not hard to imagine what she was feeling, by seeing the look on her face.

The village was expecting a "100-year flood," which doesn't mean a flood that happens every 100 years, but rather how reasonably you can expect to be prepared for such a flood. For instance, a 5-year flood means that you can reasonably expect that level of flooding to occur often, and therefore no houses should be built in any area that would be underwater during such a flood. The higher the year count, the less likely such a flood is to occur, meaning the safer it is to assume that you can build in those places.

Her house—like almost all the houses in that village—was built just outside of the 100-year flood zone, meaning she could reasonably expect her home not to flood during her lifetime. That's not a guarantee, of course, but by such estimates and probabilities we all live our lives. I know the risk is very small that I will ever be hit by lightning, so I don't need to accommodate that possibility during my daily activities. Riding a bicycle without a helmet means I increase my risk of brain damage and, though I rarely crash, I accommodate that risk by wearing one.

It took us several hours, but we accomplished what we had all come to do. We moved everything that might be destroyed by water from the ground floor to the floor above, and what we couldn't haul up the narrow stairway, because of its size or weight, we hoisted onto paving stones. It was hard work, even with so many people helping.

Not everyone was there to lift or move things. Some were there just to be there. This sort of thing happens in villages and rural areas all the time, though almost never in cities. People show up to help even if they cannot do anything physical, because physical help isn't all that's needed. You need your friends around at moments of crisis, even if they sometimes get in the way of the people hauling the heavy things. The presence of your community is how you survive such things, how you remember that disasters do not mean the end of your life, only the potential destruction of objects and possessions.

We did what we could. Not everything could be moved, and we feared that maybe we hadn't raised everything high enough off the ground. Each time I took a break I stared at the river, watching massive tree branches float past like they were ducks. Things didn't look good for the village, nor for our friend's home.

When we left, I looked at the river one more time and thought about one of the goddesses of this land. The Treverii—the Celtic people who lived in these lands and gave their name to the ancient city of Trier—revered a goddess of river crossings named Ritona. It's not difficult to understand why such a being would merit their attention and devotion. The land here is soaked through with streams and rivers that swell and diminish with the rains. To get anywhere, without bridges, you need to know where to cross them, and even to build a bridge you must know where the river is best forded, reliably shallow enough, throughout the year, to hold bridge supports.

Bridges were what the Roman conquerors needed to cross the rivers, not so much the Treverii and the other Celtic peoples here. You can ford a river with your cattle or a small cart, but you cannot ford it with a chariot or carts laden with war supplies. Any people resisting the advance of an empire that is dependent on flat surfaces for its armies would do best to rely instead on these hidden tracks across the rivers.

Far to the northeast of these lands, the pagan Lithuanians (the last pagan kingdom in Europe) built a system of hidden river and swamp crossings called *kulgrindas*. Their logic will sound familiar: Invading imperial armies (in this case, the Christian Knights Templar, charged with eradicating the last holdouts of paganism in Europe) full of armored men are slow and need roads. The pagan Lithuanians needed paths, too, but came up with an ingenious way to hide them from the Christians.

Kulgrindas are made by piling gravel, rocks, and logs over a frozen section of swamp or stream during the winter. When the ice melts, all that material sinks to the bottom, but remains covered by water. Only those who made the paths knew where they were, and thus they could ford rivers and cross otherwise impassable-seeming marshlands as if they were walking on water. Any group of Christian knights chasing after them would sink into the mud and become trapped, making them easy targets for those they were trying to slaughter.

A river ford isn't just a convenient way to get from one place to another. It is a means of protection and survival to those who know where to find it. It's evident why the Treverii worshiped a goddess of those crossings. Such a goddess is not just a being of place, but also of the knowledge of such places, a guide along secret paths to friends, to hunting grounds, to sacred sites, and to safety.

Such goddesses are no longer recognized, nor are the gods of natural forces like floods and fires. So certain have we become of our "mastery" over the world that we look at these powers as mere interruptions to be dealt with, rather than forces to be awed by, and revered.

It's hard not to think about such things after what happened. It wasn't a 100-year flood after all, but a 500-year flood. The water swept through the village up to 1.8 meters, just six centimeters below my own height.

We did all that we could possibly have done, though it was not enough. So much cannot be said regarding the larger world crisis which has intensified such flooding while unleashing other forces elsewhere. While the land where I live has been unseasonably wet, grey, and cold this summer, the land where I used to live has suffered unseasonable heat (so hot as to kill and actually cook shellfish on the beaches) and drought.

Ancient peoples are often derided, in our modern age, for their "superstitious" belief that the natural forces that caused human disasters were also spiritual. We think of them as "primitive" or "unenlightened" for treating such things as gods and shaping their lives and actions around such powers.

We forget what such a reverence actually entailed.

They made offerings to rivers and volcanoes, raised shrines to gods of fire and hearths, propitiated and remembered the dead, spoke to the beasts of forests and birds of the air as kin and neighbors. When you see the world around you as living and powerful, there is an inevitable consequence: You shape your own life with such forces in mind.

You revere the river as a goddess, and do not build upon the land she claims as her own. You revere the volcano as an ancestral mother and keep your villages out of the path of her rage. You offer prayers to the hunter-goddess of the great forest and do not take too many of her offspring for your food or too many trees from her cathedral for your own houses.

When we knew the world to be full of gods, we knew that humans were subject to the same hospitality, from nature, that we offered to each other. We were honored guests on the land, and it was best not to take too much, to shit in the springs or set fire to our surroundings, because hospitality is always conditional on the behavior of the guests.

We lost all that wisdom when empire erased our gods from memory and replaced them with its own god, first named YHVH and now named Progress. That god doesn't actually live here with us, but dwells rather outside of nature in the pale world of our ideologies. He can't show us how to cross a river to escape our enemies, or how to stop that river from claiming more land as her own.

So, we do "the best we can," knowing it's never going to be enough. The flood that drowned most of the ground floor of our friend's home could not have been predicted when the village was built, because the river had never in remembered history claimed that land as her own. Not in a hundred years, nor in any of the 800 years people have lived there. These unprecedented events will only happen more often, now, and they will happen everywhere.

I can only hope there are still some secret paths that can be forded. At least by the few who still look for those crossings, who revere those who guide us to such knowledge. Those who look in awe at the forces of nature our false god Progress has unleashed.

And I can only hope that those of us who do survive learn to live as good guests in an increasingly inhospitable world.

The Garments of the Goddesses

As I write this, the Rhine is so low that it may soon shut down to all shipping traffic. The Danube also. The Loire is so dry that you can walk across it. The Po has been that low most of this summer, revealing sunken ships and bombs from World War II. Low waters have revealed hunger stones on the Rhine, the Danube, and the Elbe. All the grassland around our house is brown. Trees have died from the drought here, and almost all the nearby stream beds are dry. A significant part of one my favorite forests in France has gone up in flames.

There are stories here, more stories than I know, more stories than I can tell. For most, these places and events may sound mythic and distant. They would have sounded that way to me before I lived here. What is happening seems unreal even as I watch it happen, as I stare at the empty streams and the parched land.

I. The Mothers of the Waters

Two weekends ago, my husband and I traveled to see members of his family in the Netherlands, his father's ancestral home. It was our second visit together, this time occasioned by the birthday of his hilarious and exceedingly lovable aunt. The land where she and her family live—and where his father was born and lived before leaving to find work in Luxembourg—is called Limburg. Most known for the city of Maastricht, and associated with a rather strong-smelling cheese cultivated with the same bacteria that causes foot odor, Limburg is one the many places within the Ardennes which somehow resisted the mono-cultural drives of Empire and Capital.

Limburg juts out south from the rest of the Netherlands as a thin peninsula into Belgian and German territory. It was once part of Belgium, just as Luxembourg was, and the land itself is unique in comparison to the rest of country. It's quite hilly, since it is part of the Eifel Mountain region. It is also at the very edge of older borders of the Ardennes, meaning we didn't actually leave the forest (or what was once all forest) to visit them.

To understand what this is like for me, think of Appalachia in the United States. Ideas about what constitutes Appalachia differ depending on who you ask or where you're from. The reason is that the Appalachian Mountains occupy a very large area of land. Many of the artificial human constructs that we call "states" occupy parts of Appalachia. The actual mountain range of Appalachia is much larger than these political definitions, and includes land occupied by Canada (Quebec, New Brunswick, and Nova Scotia, particularly) as well.

The Ardennes is similar. The way I see it, the Ardennes encompasses all of Luxembourg, most of Belgium, and parts of Germany and France. Some might disagree because the large swathe in Germany is called the Eifel, much like the question of whether the Allegheny Mountains are part of Appalachia. They are all part of the same mountain chain, but the Alleghenies is the name of a particular part of that mountain chain, a name that holds a particular meaning. Likewise, the Alps extend through Italy, France, Germany, Austria, Liechtenstein, Monaco, Slovenia, and Switzerland. Each country has its own feeling for the Alps, its own idea of what they constitute.

It's all just a question of meaning, really. Meaning assigned, culturally, to ancient landforms that pre-date humans and their meaning-making.

The distinction between the Eifel and the Ardennes is also a cultural one, going back to Roman and Frankish times. An area much larger than I described was considered the *Silva Arduenna* (Forest of Arduinna) by the Romans. Arduinna was the name of the Celtic goddess of the forests here. On the other hand, the Germanic peoples in what is called the Eifel worshiped a triplet of goddesses (the Matronae or "mothers") known as the *Matronae Aufaniae*, likely "mothers of the waters." That name, Aufaniae, is one of the suspected roots of the word Eifel. Eifel was the regional named used by the Franks to designate an administrative district (Eifelgau, which was next to Ardennengau).

Drawing hard distinctions between the Germanic and Celtic areas in this region isn't really possible. Often the assumed cultural boundaries follow political borders drawn up and imposed by the Roman Empire. The Celtic Treveri, who lived in what is both the Ardennes and southern parts of the Eifel, were adjacent to Frankish migrants who eventually also settled Treveri lands and intermixed with the people there. To the west and southwest of both these peoples were the Celtic Mediomatrici tribe. Their Romanized name means "of the middle mothers." These mothers were likely goddesses (matronae) of the rivers which passed through their land: the Meuse, the Moselle, and the Saar.

The latter two of those rivers (or mothers) join with the Rhine, which runs through lands now called the Eifel. The Meuse (or Maas in Dutch) also joins with the Rhine before flowing out to sea. However, by then the Rhine is no longer called the Rhine, but is three smaller branch rivers that split off from the mother. In fact, the Netherlands is essentially one large delta for the Rhine (and to a lesser extent the Meuse.)

The veneration of three mother figures by both Celtic and Germanic cultures is quite well attested. Neo-pagans (particularly through Wicca) derived their ahistorical idea of a triune goddess (Mother, Maiden, Crone) from the countless statues discovered of matronae while unconsciously (or perhaps intentionally) looking for a neo-pagan alternative to the Christian concept of the trinity.

There's no evidence at all that animist Celts or Germans saw these figures in this way. It is more likely that the "middle mothers" of the Mediomatrici and the Matronae Aufaniae of the Germans were the rivers and the goddesses of those rivers, in the same way that Arduinna was both a forest and the goddess of the forest. This may be difficult for our modern minds to understand because we think of pagan deities as symbols, or personified representations of a thing. We might imagine that goddesses of rivers were personifications of the river, or rulers over the river.

A more accurate description of the animist conception is that the river is a deity and also has a deity that is inseparable from it. Of course, a river isn't just one river, but hundreds and thousands of smaller rivers and streams that feed into it, each of which is also a goddess.

To get a better idea of how this works, look at the following map depicting the entire Rhine watershed, with a note demarcating where I live:

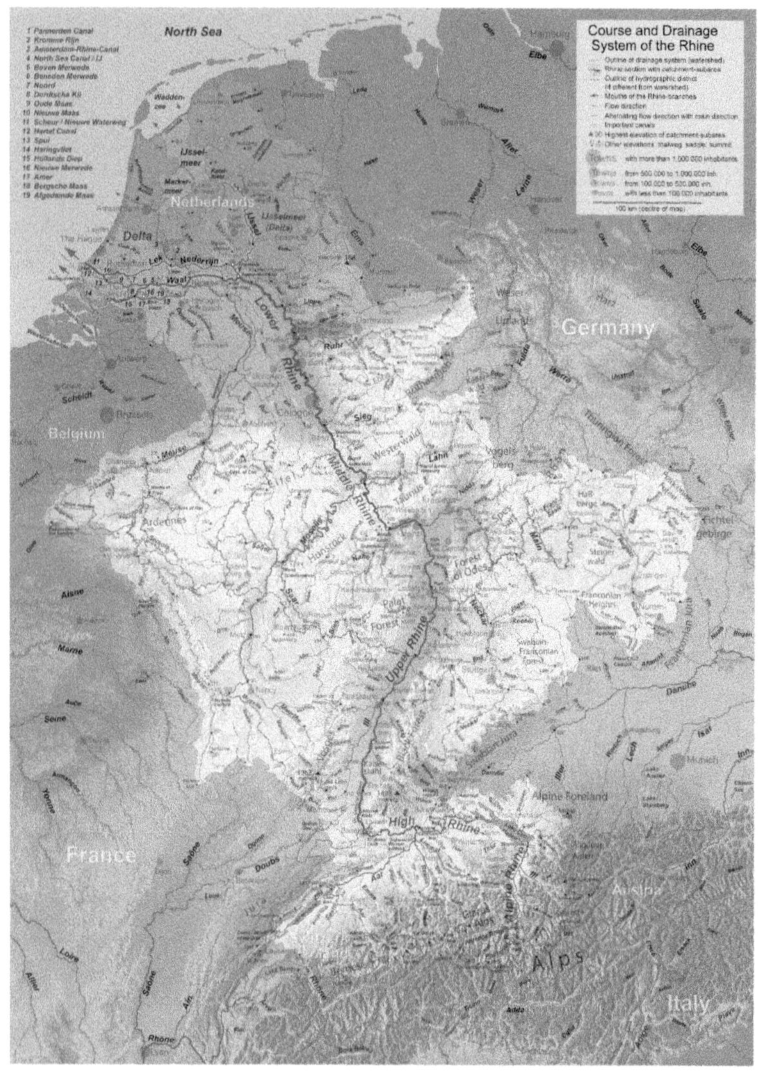
Course and Drainage
System of the Rhine
North Sea
Netherlands
Delta
IJssel-
meer
Lek
Nederrijn
Waal
Lower
Rhine
Ruhr
Sieg
Westerwald
Lahn
Middle
Rhine
Taunus
Eifel
Ardennes
Meuse
Scheldt
Belgium
Germany
Elbe
Weser
Main
Neckar
Upper Rhine
High
Rhine
Alps
Alpine Foreland
Danube
Aisne
Marne
Seine
Loire
Doubs
Saône
Rhone
France
Austria
Italy
Aar
Ill

Every river within the lighter-colored area of the map is part of the Rhine. The Rhine starts in the Alps of Switzerland and is fed by scores of "major" rivers, thousands of smaller rivers, hundreds of thousands of streams, and an uncountable number of tiny channels that only arise when it rains. One of those thousands of smaller rivers, the Syr, runs very close to my house. It's a ten-minute bike ride from my home, and I cross it twice whenever I ride to a nearby station to catch a train into Luxembourg city. When last I looked at the Syr it was not much more than a thin creek.

Across the street from my house is the Roudemerbaach, a large stream that feeds the Syr. Not far from that are the Faaschtbaach and the Aesselbaach, smaller streams that feed the Roudemerbaach just at the point where an old mill stands. That mill, where Earnest Hemingway stayed during World War II, once ground wheat for this and several other villages nearby, but it's been at least a hundred years since any of these streams were regularly strong enough to push a mill wheel. Only parts of the Roudermerbaach, where there has been reforestation, have any water right now.

The reason all these streams and rivers are empty is generally considered to be "climate change," but that's not really correct. There's been no significant rain for the last few months, and while it is true that is because of changes in the climate, there's a crucial step in between rainfall and flowing streams—the forests.

II. The Charcoal Forest and the Anthropocene

On our visit to his family in Limburg, my husband and I also visited Maastricht, a city named after the river upon which it sits (the Maas, or Meuse in French). Maastricht is not very far from a city best described as its evil Belgian twin, Liège, where the largest part of the continent's industrial revolution took place.

The story of the industrialization of Belgium is a long one, rather tragic, and very heavily influenced by English industrialists. Many of the small towns in Wallonia look an awful lot like old English mining and factory towns for precisely this reason, and they are all in deep poverty and decline. I mentioned once that you can tell immediately when you've crossed the border between Luxembourg and France—without looking at street signs—by how much trash litters the side of the road. The contrast is the same when you pass between Belgium and the Netherlands, but even more startling.

I once joked with my sister—who also lives in the Ardennes—that Belgium is the "Ohio of Europe," and she immediately agreed, laughing. I said this without malice (after all, I was born in Ohio), and I hadn't, until this trip, really understood why it felt true. Just as the deeply beautiful, ancient mountains of Appalachia were raped and then later trashed to fuel the factories of the rust belt, the Ardennes were likewise violated and for similar reasons.

That violation of the Ardennes is a little older, however. An ancient name for a particularly thick region of the *Silva Arduenna* in what is now Belgium was the *Silva Carbonaria*: the "Charcoal Forest." Precisely when it was first known as such is unclear, but the origins of the name most definitely come from the very old practice of using wood from that forest to create charcoal for iron smelting.

Charcoal burns much hotter, much longer, and much more regularly than wood, and thus was essential for early industrial iron production. In the beginning, the factories and forges of Liège were fueled by the corpses of Arduinna's cathedral giants, until coal became cheap enough to mine and transport thanks to steam engines. Liège's Dutch neighbor, Maastricht, could not compete with its capitalist iron and steel production, and was too conservative to do so anyway. Instead, Maastricht focused on pottery, textiles, and trade, none of which required nearly as much coal as the Belgian forges.

This is why there's such a difference when you cross the man-made border between Belgium and the Netherlands, and why Belgium looks so "trashed." It's because one region industrialized heavily and very, very quickly, while the other did so much more slowly and without turning all its land and people into raw material for the capitalists.

It is the same story of Appalachia, and also in England. So many resource-rich places were transformed quickly into industrial and mining wastelands. Suddenly, and for a short time, wealth flowed fast, and wages were good. Then, just as suddenly, the factories closed, the mines went dry, and the despoiled land became a trash pit and the towns places of deep despair.

There is an argument about when precisely the "Anthropocene" started. The Anthropocene is a proposed geological time period during which certain climatic trends can be read in rock layers. Each geological time division—such as the Jurassic or Mesozoic—describes periods of time during which certain kinds of life were possible, and others were not, on account of general climate conditions. Just as there are years, months, weeks, days, hours, minutes, and seconds, this kind of division proposes eons, eras, periods, epochs, and ages to mark time by the earth itself.

The Anthropocene is a proposed epoch, a period of between several thousand and a few million years, defined as a time during which human activity is the driving force affecting geological and climatic conditions. The arguments about the Anthropocene are rarely about whether the situation it describes is correct, but rather about precisely when this epoch began. Some attempt to date it to the beginning of human farming or even earlier, to the period of extinction of larger vertebrates through human hunting (mammoths, etc.). Others propose more recent events, such as the birth of human cities, colonial expansion of Europe into the Americas, the industrial revolution, or even the first atomic bomb.

Where the Anthropocene begins has more to do with ideology than objective science, and there is even a question of whether the Anthropocene should be seen as an actual epoch or as an "event." Rather than understanding the Anthropocene as long-term process, it's proposed that we see human activity as an anomalous event (or series of events) just like the "Great Oxidation Event" (during which the earth's atmosphere suddenly had a lot of oxygen, several billion years ago, and aerobic life became the dominant form on earth.)

Regardless, we generally understand that humans have deeply affected the climatic conditions of the earth through our activities, and that there have been specific moments when these affects accelerated. The industrial revolution is one such obvious acceleration, or rather a point of acceleration, and it's much more complicated than the birth of factories. The situation of the *Silva Carbonaria* in Belgium and the larger Ardennes demonstrates this quite well. Just before coal and steam became the new preferred method of fueling industrial activity, deforestation to produce charcoal had reached a dangerous peak. In fact, coal became a viable alternative precisely because charcoal production was getting more expensive: the forests were farther and farther away from urban centers because nearby forests had already been cut down.

III. Hunger Stones and Floods

A short walk from my house, crossing several currently bone-dry stream beds, there's an old forest path called rue de bois (the wood road). It was along this path that loggers hauled the massive corpses of trees to a large sawmill. Much of that wood was turned into charcoal until the forges changed to coal. Even after that switch, the sawmill kept working and the forests kept being felled, this time for lumber that would be sent down the Sûr and Moselle to merchants along the Rhine.

That's the same Rhine that is now unnavigable for most and perhaps soon all commercial shipping, just as it was in 2018. It's the same Rhine where "hunger stones" have been revealed by receding waters, warning those who see them to grieve for the coming famine.

Hunger stones are messages carved into rocks within rivers, to mark drought. Their opposites also exist: In many European cities there are stone carvings marking high water marks during floods. We tend to have a short memory for both droughts and floods alike, which is why such stones exist. They aren't prophecies, but rather historical records and warnings. A hunger stone is a reminder that when the river once got this low because of drought, things were really bad for everyone. A flood marker says the same: Once rains were so severe that the river rose this high, and everything below this level was flooded.

Speaking of floods: 44 millimeters (1 3/4 inch) of rain recently fell in the space of an hour over Paris, flooding several Metro stations. This is the sort of event one generally expects in areas subject to monsoons.

This is where memory gets very difficult. Everything around us is dry now, but a little more than a year ago, everything here was covered in water. The Rhine and its many tributaries flooded, causing many deaths and staggering economic destruction. We had flooding in our house and counted ourselves fortunate that was all we had.

The severe droughts and the severe rains are of course linked, but there is an intermediary step between the climate and its effects. That step is the forests, or rather their absence. Forests act like sponges, absorbing rainfall and slowly releasing it over a long period. The more forest a watershed region has, the less extreme the impacts of severe rain and severe drought will be. Were the original forests still here, many more of these streams would likely still have water, meaning the great rivers they feed would be less dry. Had that forest been here last year, the torrential rains would have been slowed on their way to the river by plants and soil eager to hold that water for a little while. The flooding would have been more gradual and less catastrophic.

I think this is what gets missed in the paralyzed panic about climate change. We cannot actually stop the larger processes industrialization has set into motion. It's wasted effort to pretend otherwise, and it leads to all kinds of absolutely delusional fantasies about carbon capture technology. Likewise, the hope that we could transition to nuclear in some safe way is shown ridiculous by the mere fact that these increasingly common droughts can stop nuclear power plants for months.

The "collapse" has begun and cannot be stopped. But it can be eased, and some of its effects made less catastrophic. Reforestation is one of the ways to do that, an answer that I suspect no one ever takes seriously precisely because it is so ridiculously simple. It is an answer that comes with costs, of course, not just in labor but in the conversion of residential and agricultural land back to forest land. No one will want to do that, and no one will want to pay for it, but eventually it will happen anyway.

There was a weird climatic event during the early days of American colonization that explains how this might happen. It was ugly and no one likes to talk about it, but there was an Anthropocenic reduction in atmospheric carbon dioxide that occurred before the birth of industrialization. That event is called the Orbis Spike, and it is dated to 1610. That year saw the beginning of a short but remarkable drop in atmospheric C02 around the world, as recorded in ice sheets. What happened was that a lot of carbon was suddenly sequestered (stored or captured) from the air back into plants and especially trees, because forests were suddenly growing again.

Unfortunately, there was a tragic reason for the regrowth of those forests: smallpox. Following its introduction to native populations in the Americas, smallpox killed an estimated 50 million people. They were primarily indigenous farming people, and because they died the land they farmed became forest again. In other words, the Orbis Spike event, which is one of the theoretical birthdates of the Anthropocene, was caused by widespread human death.

It's a terrible—no, hideous—truth that the mass death of humans is a boon for forests. Of course, the Orbis Spike was only temporary because industrial agriculturalists replaced those dead indigenous farmers. Had the 50 million dead been in Europe, or at least included the class of people who would later birth capitalism, perhaps the forests—and the rest of humanity—would have had a better time of it.

The point here isn't to praise colonial slaughter (far from it!) but rather to note that the forests will do quite well if a lot of us die. In other words, they'll come back regardless of whether we bring them back purposefully through reforestation or we let millions of people die because of the droughts and floods made deadlier by their absence. Either path is possible, but of course I'm hoping for the scenario without mass death. I don't know precisely how we accomplish that, but I'm pretty certain it's got everything to do with seeing the sacred again.

IV. The Forest of Fake Unicorn Horns

On the matter of the sacred: I learned today that a significant part of Brocéliande is now ash. Brocéliande, or the Fôret de Paimpont, is a relatively small woodland in Northwest France. Like many other such woodlands, it was once part of a much vaster forest that covered most of Bretagne and Normandy, and likely included still-extant forests in Central and Southwestern France.

Brocéliande is really quite small, as compared to forests in other countries, but France has so few large forests left that the 9000 hectares (35 square miles) of the Fôret de Paimpont gave it some significance. There are at least 400 fewer hectares now. From the accounts I've read, the parts that are gone are mostly along one of the major tourist routes through the forest, including the area around a fabled set of fallen megaliths called the Tomb of the Giants.

Forest fires are natural occurrences and much larger fires have been raging, throughout France, consuming much bigger areas of forest. This forest, however—well, this kind of hurts.

Brocéliande is a funny place, full of what I like to call "fake unicorn horns." I take the idea from Peter S. Beagle's *The Last Unicorn*, in which a witch who runs a traveling magical circus captures the last unicorn to be a part of the circus' spectacle. There is one problem, though—since only the pure at heart can actually see the beast as a unicorn, the witch creates a magical illusion so that people who cannot see the real one will still feel like they've seen a unicorn.

Brocéliande's fake unicorn horns are in the names of places within the forest, helpfully pointed out by overwrought mystical signs. After the Tomb of the Giants, you ascend a steep hill to Merlin's Step and Vivian's Tomb, before descending into The Valley of No Return and passing The Faerie Mirror until you come out of the forest and see a tree tastelessly painted gold. It's a tourist trap for new agers and neo-pagans, complete with a small nearby village filled with chintzy "magic" shops selling Chinese-made resin statues of fairies, polished and often mislabeled crystals, and books on energy healing.

Brocéliande was very likely a real forest, and quite likely the name of the entire forest that covered Bretagne before the Bretons arrived from Britain. If so, the Fôret de Paimpont is one of the last remaining vestiges of that forest, but none of those names—all pulled from Arthurian legend—have any connection to the places they supposedly describe. Regardless, those places have deep magic. I've (illegally, since wild camping anywhere in France is against the law) spent the night there, and done rituals there, and seen things there I can never unsee. The fake unicorn horns often point to real ones, but you must stop looking to finally see what's staring you in the face.

That's how it is, though. The sacred is often staring you in the face, and you rarely see it unless someone else points it out to you. Look at the map again, the one of the Rhine watershed. It's not just a map of a river and its myriad tributaries, but also an image of a goddess and her almost-countless younger sisters. I live within a kilometer of five of her tendrilled branches, and two kilometers from the stream they later join. That stream joins the Moselle and then joins the Rhine, but what matters most are the parts of her directly in front of my window and those other parts a short walk away. Those are the parts of her sacred self that I can see, and work for, and work along with.

All these streams once wore the forest clothing of Arduinna and laughed through her forests out towards the sea. Arduinna is mostly gone, the Ardennes a fading memory of a vast ocean of trees. Fading, but not faded, not entirely gone.

We cannot make the rains come, nor can we stop them from coming, nor can we stop industrial capitalism or climate change. We cannot undo the terrible legacy of the factories, or the slaughter of ancient forests for charcoal and later for coal mining. We cannot bring the sacred back to the entire world and undo what awful things its absence has wrought. But we can help the sacred where we are, help the forests and streams where we live, and maybe show others how to do so, too. Maybe people need some fake unicorn horns on those places for a little while, shrines and markers pointing to a sacred they cannot quite see. Many of the oldest remaining oaks in the Ardennes are host to virgin shrines where old Catholic women still go to pray. No one will cut down those trees for fear of offending God, the Church, and especially their mothers and grandmothers. So, the sacred trees are adorned with fake horns...but they remain.

This may not be a satisfying answer, but it's all I've got in me. The drought parches my soul as it parches the land, but there are still some streams flowing. They are the ones replanted with trees and river-bank plants allowed to grow wild again, streams that run through forests allowed to be themselves again rather than the "managed" areas full of lines of trees.

So, it's possible for the sacred to flow. It already happens in some places. It can happen in others. Maybe one day the goddesses will be clothed again in the raiments they once knew, and may there not be many more deaths required to make that happen.

Witches in a Crumbling Empire: Ardennes Edition

This is the text of a speech I presented at the castle of Esch-sur-Sûre in September of 2021.

Not very long ago—long as far as humans count time, but not so long as far as a tree might reckon it—the thick forests surrounding me were worshipped as a goddess. Her name was Arduinna, which was also the name of the forests she was a goddess of. It might seem strange to think of a goddess and a forest having the same name, a name we still remember when we call this land the Ardennes. It wasn't so strange to those who once lived here, though. Those people, the Treveri—from whom the city Trier takes its name—were, like all their neighbors, an animist people, people for whom the world was full of spirits, gods, and many other things we moderns now often call fairy tales or superstitions.

For the Treveri, the forests in which they lived belonged to a goddess and were, in a manner of speaking, her home. She lived in the forest, the forest was hers, and she was also the forest. Her home was full of many other things, which were also hers and part of her: wolves, lynx, bears, and aurochs, as well as trees so massive as to be the foundations of a living cathedral.

We have a tendency in our modern, secular, capitalist world to look on the ancient past—and the beliefs of those who peopled that past—as backwards, unenlightened, and savage. To think of a goddess having a forest, and a forest having a goddess may perhaps seem silly, incomprehensible, a useless myth.

Yet the forest of Arduinna was once full of animals that have also become mythic to us. It has been 150 years since a lynx was last was seen in Luxembourg, a millennium since a bear was anywhere near the Ardennes, and the last aurochs on earth died almost 400 years ago. Of all those mythic creatures, only the wolf has returned, seen last year 3 kilometers away from where the "last wolf" was killed in 1893.

What happened to the animals of Arduinna's forest has happened to animals and plants across the world, whether they are in forests, in fields, or in the oceans. Last century, 500 species went extinct. In 2020 alone, another 15 disappeared forever. These extinctions, which are accelerating and occur at roughly 1000 times the "natural extinction rate," are primarily due to human activity. In many cases, such extinctions have been the result of habitat loss: humans destroying or radically changing the places where those beings lived. In some cases, especially those of large mammals, this disappearance is due to over-hunting. And in more and more cases, human-caused climate change has led to the irrevocable disappearance of a species from the earth.

About that goddess, Arduinna... From what we know of her, she was associated with hunting and revered in high places. The Romans, as was their imperial habit, renamed her after their own huntress god, Diana. Later, the Franks who settled these lands and mixed with the Treveri saw in Arduinna a likeness to Freya. For all three peoples, though, the thick, nearly impenetrable forest—densely populated with animals that are no longer here—was sacred, as was the goddess who made the forest her home.

The Ardennes Forest, deeply diminished in respect to its former spread—a spread so thick and profound that early Christian missionaries wrote despairingly of it—was once part of a much larger forest, the Horcinian. The Schwarzwald in Germany and the Ardennes were once connected to each other, part of the same forest. That forest stretched far west, past the Vosges into the Morvennes in Central France, and east all the way to the largest remaining forest of Europe, the Białowieska. There are not many forests left, and none of them are connected to each other any longer.

A certain thing happens when you believe a forest is a god or goddess, that a god or goddess lives there, and that the forest belongs to them, rather than to humans. What happens is that you see the forest as sacred—meaning something set apart from the everyday human realm—and you treat the forest as such. Just as with other sacred things, you don't use it too much, you don't destroy it, you take care of it, and you don't let others destroy it.

The river which runs past this castle also belonged to a goddess, and was itself a goddess. The Treveri knew many such goddesses, including a goddess of the crossing of rivers. Her name is Ritona, meaning "she of the fordings."

Rivers are peculiar things. They are a source of life—of food and water. They are also a source of protection, acting as a natural barrier against imperial armies who require bridges to cross them. Like other sacred things, however, they have their own interests. Not long ago, this river—like all the other rivers throughout this land—flooded her banks during heavy rains.

Ancient animist, pagan peoples believed that unusual weather patterns and natural disasters were a sign of anger from the gods, a way of showing their displeasure at the actions of humans. We dismiss such ideas as superstitious and unscientific, yet those rains which swelled these rivers, flooding homes, sweeping away property, and ending lives, are actually, scientifically, the fault of humans.

The increased temperature of the earth on account of our industrial activity—our "modern" way of living—caused the melting of large fields of ice in the Arctic. This melt changed ocean currents that regulate the temperature here in Europe as well as along America's Eastern Seaboard. This led to what climate scientists called "the polar vortex" escaping the Arctic and freezing many American states last winter. This same disruption caused catastrophic droughts and heat waves which cooked shellfish on the beaches, while also causing the heavy rains we saw here in the Ardennes and along the Rhine.

In light of all this, the ancient animist belief that natural disasters are linked to human actions suddenly sounds pretty reasonable. Droughts, famines, floods, and plagues were all seen as signs of divine displeasure at human actions, and we are living in a time when such things are all occurring at increasing rates. Because I make a habit of not speaking about a certain plague now sweeping the world, I'll mention a much smaller one that I suffered myself.

Last year, when I was wandering one of the many fragments of Arduinna's forests—one filled with magnificent oaks, a tree particularly sacred to the Celtic and Germanic peoples who populated this land—three caterpillars happened to land on my neck. Being new to this land, I thought nothing about it until later that night when my body was so covered with red welts that I could not move.

Those caterpillars were Oak Processionary Spinners. Native to the remnants of Turkish forests, they were brought here through the vector of modern trade, to feed our industrial hunger for oak wood. Having felled the vast majority of oaks in the Ardennes, merchants paid for the felling and importation of Turkish oaks. Along with those oaks came the caterpillars. As with so many other disasters, this is something we humans did, a consequence of our actions.

The ancestors of this land understood this perhaps better than we do: What humans do to nature has consequences. When people ask me what it means to be a pagan now, I point to this. I point to the floodings, to the droughts, to the melting icecaps, to the extinctions, to the plagues. And then I point to what was once believed in these lands—and in fact every land on earth—that nature is sacred, it is full of gods and goddesses, and treating it otherwise results in sorrow, pain, and misery for humans.

It took a very long time for humans to lose these beliefs. Sometimes I read the accounts of Christian missionaries and laugh at their frustration. St. Hubertus, for example, the patron saint of hunters and called "the apostle of the Ardennes," is said to have sat on a tall pole for months or perhaps years in protest of the locals' belief in Arduinna (whom the Catholic writers mistook for the Roman Diana). St. Boniface railed against the backwardness of Frankish peoples treating oaks as gods, whining repeatedly to multiple popes about how difficult it was to convince them that they were just trees.

When did pagan beliefs die here? It's unclear, and it's not certain they died completely, despite the witch-hunts that swept through this and every other country in Europe. While many write off the hysteria over witches as merely a superstitious moment in our progress toward modern enlightenment, the Marxist Feminist writer Silvia Federici has shown that the witch-hunts were actually a crucial step in the creation of industrial capitalism. Witches, who were primarily but not entirely women, were often people whose work and knowledge were a continuation of that older way of seeing the world. To convince us all that nature was not sacred, we had to first be convinced that the people who believed so were evil and should be murdered.

Put another way, the so-called Enlightenment—which is better described as the birth of the mechanistic worldview—was born at the witch's stake. It was also born on the factory floor, those "satanic mills" where nature was no longer sacred, and neither was human life. Humans became cogs in a machine, a machine that constantly vomited into the air black coal smoke and something blacker yet invisible: carbon dioxide.

That's the stuff, of course, which has caused all the divine retribution we call "catastrophic climate change" or "global warming." While belief in the power of invisible things is usually associated with superstition—a kind of magical thinking that the witch-hunts, the age of reason, and the industrial disenchantment of the world supposedly eradicated forever—we all find ourselves true believers again.

Like the renaissance alchemists, we now trace the effects of etheric substances produced in the alembics of our motors, our engines, our power plants. We call this science, and shake our heads in shame at those who believed spirits populated the air, the rivers, the forests, and all those other parts of nature now suffering the effects of this invisible force. The witches were killed to silence such beliefs yet here, now, our world—including the human world—is drowning and burning, just as the witches did.

These are dark words, no easier to hear than they are for me to speak. We are killing ourselves by killing nature, which is to say the same thing. What our supposedly superstitious, backwards, and primitive ancestors knew was that you cannot speak of what lives in the world as separate from the world itself. Just as the goddess Arduinna lived in these forests around us and also was these forests, just as these rivers had goddesses but were also goddesses themselves, we humans live in nature, and we are nature.

Now, of course, we see ourselves as separate from nature and call ourselves "modern." We have smartphones yet have become dumb to the wisdom calling us from the earth. We have a global network of orbital satellites transmitting cute cat photos and vapid opinions directly into our pockets, yet we can no longer hear the songs of the stars or the guidance of the moon.

Silvia Federici has shown us that to accomplish this separation, the witches had to be burned. They were burned because they refused to be modern, just as indigenous people were colonized, re-educated, converted, and often slaughtered because they held to their old ways. In both cases, it was the beliefs that had to be destroyed, beliefs embodied in the flesh of peoples for whom an older way of relating to the world simply made more sense.

We stopped believing in forest goddesses so that the forests could become just wood to us. We stopped believing in rivers as goddesses so they could be dammed, rechanneled, and polluted according to our will. We stopped believing in humans as part of nature so that we could turn them into machines. Workers became mere, interchangeable cogs in the machinery of the mills and the mines that create all that we embrace as modern.

That "modern" is what is killing us. Whether you believe in gods or not, the retribution of the earth—which our pagan, animist ancestors believed would result from the abuse of engodded nature—is happening regardless.

These are dark words, so I will tell you of something else, something less dark, something that gives me relentless hope and is the goal of all my work: There are still witches, and there are still gods. Those ancient beliefs we discarded and thought extinct are still here, and often in plain sight.

Every year, in Luxembourg and throughout the Ardennes, an ancient ritual is enacted. It is a ritual the Treveri ancestors of this land knew, as did many other Celtic peoples to the north, the east, and the south of here. It is a ritual the Frankish peoples who came later to these lands recognized immediately, because it was a ritual practiced by Germanic peoples as well.

That ritual is called the *Buergbrennen*. Celebrated now as a village festival connected to the Catholic Church, people gather wood and straw and set them alight to burn away the winter.

The Christian missionaries, who brought with them a new belief about the world, faced an impossible task: how do you convince people to change their ways, to stop doing the things they've done for thousands of years? One might as well try to convince a forest to stop being a forest, or a river to stop being a river.

Eventually they learned a trick, one the Roman Empire was quite good at. Rather than destroying every ancient thing, you just rename them. That is how the Romans renamed shrines to Arduinna as shrines to Diana, and how the missionaries renamed these ancient pagan fires, the *Buergbrennen*, as Christian celebrations.

Just as a forest doesn't stop being a forest if you call it something else, nor does a river stop being a river just because you call it a lake, neither did these pagan rituals stop being rituals just because they were now called Catholic. Enter any Catholic church in Europe and you'll see quite a lot of pagan gods still hanging around. Of course, they've all got new names now: Cernunnos is now called St. Hubertus, Hermes is now called St. Expedite. Odin and Gwyn ap Nudd still ride their wild hunt across the winter skies, but they're now called St. Nicholas and bring presents rather than leading the souls of the dead to their homes. Ancient hilltop shrines to goddesses still have statues upon them, though they are now named Mary and dressed in imperial garb.

It's not so easy to kill a belief in a god. It's much simpler to hide them in plain sight, to re-brand them just as we've re-branded alchemy as chemistry and the vengeance of nature gods as climate change. The gods never went away, nor did the witches.

Witches were not what the judges and inquisitors claimed them to be. They were not women stealing children for sacrifice to infernal spirits, but rather women still living as we all once did. Healing themselves and others with gifts from the forests, ending unsafe or unwanted pregnancies with those same gifts. Whispering prayers and incantations, perhaps, but to spirits and gods who were woven into the land itself, rather than sitting upon a distant throne judging the acts of men. Timing their lives according to the moon and the seasons, rather than the imposed discipline of factory and machine time.

People everywhere have always done such things, and still do. We often look to indigenous societies to find the wisdom we have lost, yet that same wisdom speaks from the very trees which surround this place. There are still people in the Ardennes whispering Arduinna's name, just as there are people elsewhere whispering the names of others. I know of many such people, many of them women, many of them practicing witchcraft as the ancients once did.

The last decade has seen an explosion of interest in witchcraft, and in other, older kinds of relationship to the earth. Permaculture—which is a new name for an indigenous way of raising plants—has become a large movement alongside interest in homesteading, traditional crafting, and other more stable ways of living in the world.

Artistic exploration of this kind of relationship to the land has also grown significantly. I know of more and more artists and musicians, every year, who are weaving songs and stories from the land, channeling a wisdom that we thought was lost. I think of one such woman, born in this land and now living in Norway, practicing the animist witchcraft known as *Seidr* while tapping birch trees for sugar, raising food as we all once did, and channeling the wisdom of that land into song for the rest of us to hear.

That such interest in animism, in paganism, in witchcraft, and in traditional ways of living has increased while climate disruptions have accelerated is no mere coincidence. I suspect we will see more of this, more of a desire to return to what we thought was lost. More of us will see the forests and rivers as sacred again, as beings to be venerated and respected rather than trashed and exploited.

Whether it is too late or not, I do not know. I only know—as I am sure you all know as well—that our world is dying and the modern will soon go away. Whether this ends the way all empires end, with violence, famine, and despair, or whether it will end as rituals often end, with new wisdom and insight, I also do not know.

I know one thing, though. Neither the gods nor the witches ever really went away.

Witch Bottles, Hell Fire, and the "True Believer"

It was a Saturday. I was making lasagna, occasionally glancing through the kitchen window at the man I love as he dug a massive hole for a tree he was transplanting. I was just about to put the lasagna in the oven when he came upstairs and said, "Hey, look at this."

I almost dropped the lasagna on the floor.

"Uh—" I stuttered, suddenly panicked, having one of those really urgent feelings I've come to recognize as something from elsewhere.

"I found it in the garden. It's really, really old."

I think the way I spoke to him then was the closest I've ever come to sounding like a rude, demanding jerk. "Can I have that?" I don't think I spoke those words as a question.

"Yes, it's for you. As soon as I saw it, I knew you should have it."

"Thanks," I said, really curtly, and then proceeded to say "oh fuck" to myself several times while he cleaned up.

I.

Only a hundred or so years after the printing press was developed, a book was published that became a must-have for the new class of well-off artisans and landowners who eventually became the bourgeoisie in Europe. Next to printed editions of the Bible, the book you were most likely to find displayed proudly on a shelf was *The Great Albert.*

The Great Albert, or more specifically *Liber Secretorum Alberti Magni Virtutibus Herbarum, Lapidum et Animalium Quorumdam*, was a compilation of magical texts attributed to Albertus Magnus, a 13th-century monk who produced a large body of alchemical and esoteric works. *The Great Albert* was a household reference text for magic, for folk cures, and especially for prayers and charms against certain maladies with either magical or natural origins.

The book was originally in Latin, and translated initially into German, later French, and then English. I first learned of the book's existence two years ago, when a copy was placed in my hands. The person who owned it didn't know what it was. He collected antique things in general with the hope of making a fortune on the resale of something valuable, though most of what he had accumulated was probably just trash. The version he had was in Latin and was dated from the mid 1600's, bound in goatskin and scrawled with notes throughout. The markings reduced its value, nevertheless he was in possession of a book worth several thousand euros, but he didn't know it yet.

My Latin is awful. I took two years of it in high school, just enough to understand the roots of most Romance-language words and that I'm really bad at declensions. Regardless, I knew enough to translate the title page and tell him what he had. After a quick internet search for prices, he promptly took the book out of my hands and returned it to a locked chest.

Books such as *The Great Albert* became a kind of home reference guide for many households, popular not just for their esoterica but also for their practical advice, including how to deal with *malefica,* that is, witchcraft. Charms and incantations steeped in Christian language, often written as prayers, could cure and protect against any ailment thought to come from the devil or those who consorted with him. While such a worldview might seem bizarre, our current theories on virus transmission and infectious diseases stem from a belief that invisible things—only viewable by means of certain mechanics—cause illness. Which isn't all that different from what they believed. It's just that we're pretty sure we're right, now, and that they were wrong then.

II.

The house my partner was born in, and in which he still lives, is quite old. We're not certain exactly how old, because we're not certain which version of the house was the original.

It's located in the Ardennes, in a valley with several streams running through it. Centuries ago—and up until the late 1900s—there was a mill here along one of those streams, which belonged to the lord who held title to this land. At some point in the 17th century, or as late as the middle of the 18th century, a century or two after the end of feudalism here, the lord converted old houses into servants' quarters. One of those quarters was also the washing house. A brook ran past the building (it's been diverted slightly now to just across the street), which also had a deep well and was next to a natural spring, thus making it the perfect place for a washing house (two sources of clean water, one source of strong current).

This is where the laundry was done. My partner's mother is the descendant of one of the village washing-women who was allowed to live in the building as payment for her work. Eventually the lord fell to ruin, but several generations of washing-women continued to live in the house, which became theirs.

My partner's mother was born in this house and lived here her entire life (still does—when my partner took over the house he built a large apartment for her on the first floor, roughly where the very original living quarters were). So, the house has an unbroken matrilineal line of washing-women (my partner's mother's profession for quite some time as well) extending back several centuries. One of those women, sometime in the last few hundred years, buried a small, corked apothecary bottle with some hair in it in the yard.

They're called witch bottles, one of the many remedies prescribed by the popular grimoires of Europe to deal with *malefica*. A witch bottle involves what's called apotropaic magic—basically, anything meant to ward off, deflect, or redirect bad luck or evil influence. "Knocking on wood" is this sort of magic, as is one of the two versions of finger crossings. Talismans against the evil eye (including flying penises) are apotropaic magic, as are the gargoyles on churches.

A witch bottle functions in a slightly different way than most such wards because it is meant to act as a decoy. The basics of creating one are pretty simple: You put hair, fingernails, or other easily-gotten bits of your own body into the bottle, along with a piece of iron. Then you piss in it (most traditional) or add other things, cork it, and bury it either in your garden or in the foundation of your house.

The bottle acts as a decoy, or a magical sink. Once it is in place, the majority of general or specific ill-will directed at you cannot find its target, as there is something redirecting that ill-will or "absorbing" it. Of course, a skilled magician or a very vindictive witch would be able to compensate for this, but most people who hate you don't have those skills.

III.

That first night, I did nothing with the bottle my partner found in the garden. I was tired and distracted, and anyway I wasn't fully certain it actually was a witch bottle. It had the elements of one, but I've learned not to rush to conclusions about a magical object until I've had time to think about other options as well. The next day I still wasn't fully certain, and so I kept the bottle in a neutral place and promptly got distracted.

I remember a weird dream that night, just before sleeping. Someone was telling me that I was dying. They weren't very urgent about it, more like an off-handed mention. My response was just as neutral: "Oh, yeah, of course. But I'll be alive tomorrow, so it won't be tonight."

The person, who was my grandfather, just shrugged, and that was the end of the dream.

The next morning, I woke up incredibly groggy and disoriented. My partner was already awake, so I stumbled into the kitchen where he looked much more serious than he normally does on Monday mornings.

"Do you smell the smoke?" he asked. And that was when I understood why I was so groggy.

Before we had gone to sleep, he had decided to put a final coat of wood varnish on an oak table, and then disposed of the used rag in a way this obsessively meticulous man never had before: he placed it in a plastic bag in a storage room, amongst other plastic bags.

Varnish-soaked rags heat up when they dry. If they dry too quickly and are touching any flammable surface, they will ignite, which is what this rag did. It then burned through the other plastic bags while we slept, filling the house with a thick black smoke that took days to finally dissipate.

There were two particularly odd things about that night. Neither the smoke nor carbon monoxide alarms triggered. We tested them both that morning and they were working. Also, the fire had burned most of the night, but not all of it. It hadn't spread, despite the fact that there were even more flammable items touching those bags.

If you're esoterically minded, you can probably guess what I did next. I cleared out the bottle (the cork had mostly rotted away and it was no longer sealed). I burned what was inside, mostly for extra confirmation that the dirty clump inside it was hair (it was, according to the smell as it burned). The rest of what I did is also guessable, but those details are for me.

Something else happened around this time, by the way. My partner came down with what in German is called *Höllenfeuer*—hell fire. *Höllenfeuer* is shingles, albeit a specific variant of it. The virus that causes chickenpox hides in the nervous system and lies dormant there for most of your life (your entire life, if you're lucky). However, during moments of extreme stress or in the case of a compromised immune system, it re-emerges and attacks the specific nerve where it had been hiding.

Höllenfeuer is shingles in the sciatic nerve. Imagine if you will the worse sciatica of your life. And then add with it the sensation that your leg is being alternatively sawed off and boiled. And then add a terrifying rash. That's *Höllenfeuer.*

The pain was horrific, and he needed several months to heal. The time off from work did him well, though, which is the other point here. Both incidents (the fire and the hellfire) can just as easily be ascribed to the stress of work as to an ancient glass bottle he found buried deep in the earth.

IV.

When you start to "do" magic, by which I mean when you accept the framework of magic as a potential explanation for things, there's a moment where it's possible to go completely mad. The Chinese have a name for it. It's *zou huo ru mo*, or "qigong deviation," a term that describes a psychological disorder that seems to occur in the beginning stages of some martial arts training. Instead of learning to channel certain energies, you are overtaken by them. You become delusional, obsessive, paranoid, suffer from megalomania, and experience strange sensations that have no external cause.

It's thought to occur when something goes wrong with the early training, when there is some interruption or lack of guidance. And it's curable, but the cure usually requires that the afflicted person stay away from such practices for a while, or possibly forever. Although the condition is acknowledged in the West, it's usually attributed to schizophrenia or other mental conditions that were triggered during the training.

When someone starts to practice magic—or even to read about magic—and certain "supernatural" things begin to happen or, like Jung, they experience "synchronicity" (apparent repetition, as if the world around you is suddenly orchestrated), that experience can be either humbling and liberating or terrifyingly destabilizing. The former saves you. The latter makes you a complete madman, at least for a little while.

In the people that I know for whom this "deviation" lasted more than a day or two (I think it actually happens to everyone for a brief moment but passes as soon as you regain yourself), the experience became one of manic certainty. Spirits and gods and magics are everywhere and in everything: Now that you see them, you feel you hold the key to the universe. If you keep believing this you'll exhaust yourself, at best or, at worst, you'll never recover and wreak havoc on your own life and the lives of others.

Another way of putting it is that you suddenly find a framework that changes your world, and you lose yourself to it. This "deviation" isn't really all that different from the "true believer" syndrome you see in Christian conversions, or what happens when someone gets "woke" or "red-pilled." Jesus or Judith Butler or Alex Jones has shown you the man behind the curtain, the truth beneath the rose, the glory beyond the cross, and you have finally found your one purpose in life.

From what I have read about people who experienced qigong deviation, the problem appears to be the same as in the Western versions of the phenomenon. Specifically, some center of the self is displaced. Put another way, your will or agency is diminished, replaced by a sense of externality that overwhelms you. Everything becomes grand narrative, and in the Western versions (where dualism is the core foundation of even secular frameworks), demons or the Illuminati or the patriarchy or Jews or white supremacy or infidels or cis-heterosexuals are actively trying to destroy you. You think you've just found the key to stopping them, and all you need to do is enlist others into your cosmic crusade.

Of course, many people—the majority, I'd argue—encounter these frameworks and don't lose themselves to them. They regain some sense of themselves quickly and see the framework as just a framework. A useful one, a meaningful one, perhaps a liberating one. But only one framework.

That's how I could stare at the bottle in my partner's hand, experience the subsequent incidents, know about the history and use of witch bottles, get confirmation from my partner's mother that her elders were interested in such things, even test the contents, yet still hold in my head the very likely possibility that it was just a discarded bottle and that the fire and hell fire were just effects of my partner's work stress.

In fact, that's the only way to do magic. You have to hold multiple frameworks in your head, otherwise you'll miss things. This is not all that different from what the people who lived here did before Christianity swept through. They invoked multiple gods—including foreign gods—to make sure that they were dealing correctly with all potential influences. This is what Catholic bishops, monks, and even a few popes did as well.

It's also the only way to avoid being driven to ideological madness. I'm a Marxist, yes. But I'm also a Pagan. And an anarchist. And sometimes a Classic Liberal. Sometimes I'm more like a European conservative than I'd rather explain to most people. Often, I can understand why Republicans and Right Libertarians have the views they do. Maybe craziest of all, I'm mostly not even political.

The ability to hold several frameworks in your head, and sift through them to see how each might apply to a situation, isn't a supernatural or superhuman trait. It's the core requisite of sanity. People who cannot sift through their frameworks or who wield the same one repeatedly, no matter the situation, are a lot like the person who keeps ringing a doorbell long after it's obvious that nobody is home. Yes, the doorbell works. But ringing it only results in an open door under certain conditions and at certain times.

This is how political movements go from being potentially liberating to being absolutely fucking insane. They are incomplete frameworks (there is no such thing as a complete framework), useful in some cases and completely useless in others. The more that a framework is applied to things it cannot accurately describe, the more fragile that framework gets and the more unstable the person wielding it becomes.

The only way to deal with this problem is the same as the remedy for qigong deviation and other such problems: Step back from such frameworks completely, and let yourself reset. You might come back to them later. If so, you'll be returning with a new perspective, one that helps you maintain your agency and make such frameworks more useful. Or maybe you'll realize that they were never useful at all.

Either way, you'll regain yourself, and that's a deep and powerful magic.

The Tyranny of Machine Meaning

I.

Almost a decade ago, during a time in which my entire life was in the process of radical change, I went on a backpacking trip across Europe. It was a trip, alone, to ancient pagan sites and places of particular meaning to me. It was my first such journey without a companion, and the first long period of time, during my adult years, that I was completely alone with my own thoughts.

No one else was with me to mediate my experience. Smartphones were just becoming a "thing" at the moment, but I didn't have one, nor had I a laptop or even a watch. I was using paper maps and guidebooks to find my way, with no GPS or any internet service to rely upon.

I did have one modern item, however: a camera, gifted by a friend along with a request that I "use it well." In the first few days of that trip, I did use it, and quite often. I was in a state of wonder, a state you can easily cultivate in new places and especially in particularly beautiful environments. Everything seemed to me magical, enchanted, breathtaking, and I took relentless photos of the things I saw.

It was perhaps the fifth or sixth day of that trip, hiking along the rugged coastline of Brittany after wandering through ancient standing stone alignments, that I lost the camera. After hours of panic, self-berating, and long retracing of my steps to try to find it again, I eventually understood this was the best thing that ever happened to me.

This is how I wrote about it afterwards:

> I wonder, though. Did some higher part of myself leave it on the rocks on purpose? Or did I leave it at the chapel? Its loss has actually been a very good thing for me. Here's why: I'd see something profound, beautiful, breathtaking, otherworldly, and immediately fumble for my camera, snap a couple of photos, check to see if I'd caught the image right, and then put it away and walk on.
>
> That is, I stopped seeing things, except to see them for others. I realized this just as the sun was setting, just as I knew I had no hope of getting back before dark. I sat on a rock, frustrated, tired, and found myself seeing something unimaginable in its beauty.
>
> The sun set over the bay, brilliant and dark hues of purples, violets, blues mixing with crimson reflecting off the water of the bay (the tide had come in fully now). Greens of seaweed floated like islands upon the water, and silver danced in the waves where the last whites of the sun hit. The stones of the shore were black, but also dun, as was the sand, though giving off a yellow-gold that seemed like trapped sunlight from the warm day.
>
> I cried, but not from sadness.

I know others have had this sort of experience. When you attempt to capture a vision, or a moment, or an experience with technology, you are no longer in the present. That is, you actually kill the experience by trying to capture it, just like picking a beautiful flower separates it from the earth which gives it life.

II.

Included in a released trove of "whistleblower" documents regarding Facebook were internal studies showing the deleterious effects of Instagram use on teenage girls. Some have pointed out that the studies themselves are not very scientific, and that even the respondents reported that they didn't think they should stop using Instagram. This misses the point, however: We don't really have a good way of measuring the effects of social media on how we conceive of ourselves, despite intuitively understanding that it's not good for us.

I know an Instagram "Influencer," by the way. That's a meaningless term, of course: An Influencer is just someone with an inhumanly large following on that social media platform—over 20,000 people (and sometimes in the low millions). What distinguishes an Influencer from any other user is precisely their number of followers. I used Instagram often for a few years and accumulated under 2,000 followers, while this person used it for even less time and accumulated 50 times that amount (100,000).

To accumulate that kind of following, you need to post very, very often. Not only that, but you also need to be particularly good at using hashtags and choosing filters for your photos and videos that evoke certain moods. And, of course, you need to be really good at taking evocative and viral photos. You can purchase large numbers of followers, something that many of the earliest Influencers did. These are mostly bulk packages of bot accounts created in "bot farms," hundreds and thousands of refurbished phones (and computers running emulator programs) with Facebook and Instagram accounts, each programmed with subroutines to mimic actual human use.

Once Facebook identified this manipulation they began to crack down on it, but they were never fully successful. Twitter, likewise, has been unable to deal with the bot problem. There was another "cheat" to gain large followings on Instagram as well. For a relatively small fee, compared to the potential income becoming an Influencer can generate, a user could pay a service to follow and then unfollow thousands of other users. Typically, when someone receives a follow, they follow that account back. Since the app does not notify you of unfollows, you don't symmetrically unfollow those who have unfollowed you, allowing someone using this service to gain a massive audience very quickly.

With the exception of people who were already celebrities for other reasons, most Instagram Influencers achieved their status through one of these methods of manipulation (if not both). Now that the company that runs Instagram has implemented algorithms to limit this kind of cheating, it's nearly impossible to become an Influencer.

It's a bit like the way capital works. Both Capital and Influence only have "value" when they are rare. That is why the early capitalists, who accumulated mass amounts of wealth, later created laws to prevent others from doing the same thing. Both states and revolutions do this as well, quickly outlawing the founding violence through which they initially gained power to prevent others from competing with their authority.

Now, this Influencer that I know personally? I don't know if you can call what we are "friends," though I definitely enjoy this person's presence when they aren't on their phone. That's really rare, though.

We've been to several public events together; dinners, celebrations, parties, those sorts of things. Though this person is present, they are never actually there, but rather constantly taking photos and videos of the things around them, editing, re-shooting. Several times I've watched this person re-arrange tables or direct others to do things to create an "experience" for Instagram. Such moments, after editing and filtering, with the correct selection of hashtags, get thousands and thousands of "likes."

But it's all fake. Looking through the Instagram posts this person creates, from events at which I was present, there is such a wild disconnect between what they present and what actually happened that it all feels quite shocking. Each post is an idealized version of the event and the environment, plastic and hollow but perfectly framed for an audience none of us will ever meet.

The same thing doubtless occurs on all other Influencer accounts. When I actively used Instagram, I followed quite a few of them (all accounts that followed me back initially then quickly unfollowed), and often stared in bewilderment at how perfect their lives looked. At first, I would actively remind myself that their photos were staged, that the enchanting visions they presented were heavily filtered, arranged, and of course selected from scores of less-than-perfect photos they later discarded. Yet even actively approaching these images with a critical eye, eventually I started to see them as real, as authentic representations of someone else's life.

III.

One of the key mechanisms of social identity is comparison. We compare ourselves constantly to others, noting similarities and differences and adjusting our sense of self accordingly. We do this and we need to do this. At the most basic level of human experience, knowing what the people around us are feeling, wearing, or looking like helps us understand our place in social groups. "Reading the room" is a core social skill most of us learn to cultivate in our teenage years and, to do so, we learn to read others.

Comparing ourselves to images rather than to people is much less reliable, of course. We all know, intellectually, why we should not do that, but without constant and active effort to disenchant those images, we fall into such comparison regardless. That Influencer I wrote of constantly compares themself to others and struggles more, I think, than anyone I have ever met with deep self-hatred, fragile self-esteem, and the physical torment of an eating disorder.

I know of another such person, a friend, a man with an incredible physique achieved through attentive gym work. He is someone whom I and many others looked to for advice and encouragement about body transformation. He deleted all his social media accounts after recovering from an attempted suicide, explaining to us that he realized Instagram was killing his self-esteem and would eventually kill him if he didn't stop using it.

These two people I mention are both adults, fully "individuated," with successful careers and very stable living situations. They're not teenage girls, by which I mean they have had a lot more time to develop their sense of self than an adolescent woman has.

I was never a teenage girl, so I cannot fully imagine what it must be like for them, but I know from my own adolescence that hatred of my body was pretty much a constant theme. Based on what many women I know have told me about their youth and adulthood, it feels safe to say it's even worse for them than it ever was for me.

I didn't have social media back then (it didn't exist), and I wonder how much worse my life might have been had it existed. I could only compare myself to the other boys at school and the obviously idealized men on television (which I stopped watching completely at 13). There were no men or women in my life at that time who told me that being a body was just a human thing that we all experience, or that comparison needs to be balanced with a strong sense of independence and will.

Even now, understanding this truth, I am often under the thrall of the idealized image that we create of ourselves and our lives through social media, even after I stopped looking at the Feeds.

In his essay, "The Work of Art in the Age of Mechanical Reproduction," the Marxist writer Walter Benjamin explored the way that industrialization changed our understanding of art, especially through the mass production of the camera and its products, the photograph and the moving film. One of his most profound (and least cited) insights draws parallels between the totalitarian drive of fascism and the influence of mechanical reproduction.

> The growing proletarianization of modern man and the increasing formation of masses are two aspects of the same process. Fascism attempts to organize the newly created proletarian masses without affecting the property structure which the masses strive to eliminate. Fascism sees its salvation in giving these masses not their right, but instead a chance to express themselves.

Benjamin, as well as others who later built on his work, saw the fascist drive not as a "reactionary" or conservative backlash to progress and industrial society, but rather as an aspect of the machine itself. Instead of the more popular conception of fascism as a revolt against social progress and equality, fascism for Benjamin was a re-channeling of lower-class desires away from revolution and back into the capitalist order.

It is not at all a stretch to suggest that the "chance to express themselves" he mentions is fulfilled in the idealized reproduction represented by Instagram and other platforms (TikTok, Snapchat, etc.). In social media reproduction of "art," we turn every part of our life into a product, a commodity to be exchanged and a value upon which corporations can capitalize. The Influencer, in particular, becomes a node of aesthetic production, highly sought-after for commercial partnerships in exchange for free products or cash payments, while the rest of us unconsciously mimic their poses and devalue our own lives because they do not compare to what we see.

What is being produced, reproduced, and channeled here is the expression of human desire for meaning. Industrial society alienates us not only from each other but also from our own selves and our capacity to value (that is, attach meaning to something), and social media offers us, in its place, only the exchange of other people's valuing.

That is, we are offered only the ability to express ourselves as a poor replacement for our desire and right to shape the world. With that expression comes comparison, not to other humans but to idealized, commodified, and fully mediated reproductions of lives that don't actually exist. Jean Baudrillard, basing his work on Walter Benjamin's essay, called these simulacra—copies for which an original no longer exists—and saw this as the dominant mode of capitalist control of human meaning and the inescapable consequence of technology.

IV.

We now know that simulacra are making people suicidal.

We already knew this, of course. We know it each time we spend too long on social media and find that we feel shitty about ourselves. Others have it better, have more beautiful bodies and more fulfilling lives, are eating better meals, going on better vacations, posing more often with happier-looking friends on terraces overlooking more breathtaking vistas than we ever see outside our own windows. The men look more masculine than we will ever be, the women more feminine. Their lives and bookshelves are fuller, their teeth and skin more pleasing, their lovers and families more caring and joyful than anything we could ever hope to have.

The moment you turn all that off, however, you can finally start to see the world around you for what it truly is. When I lost my camera on a cliff on a wild coastline, I finally noticed the beauty screaming for my attention. When I stopped letting the algorithms of the social media Feeds decide for me what was meaningful, I finally remembered that meaning is something I have always held in my hands.

Walter Benjamin saw machine meaning as a core aspect of fascism, a key tool to make us forget we have the right to make the world ourselves. Such a view runs completely counter to the way liberals and progressives understand fascism, since for them the machine itself liberates humans from the terror of the Real. At best, liberals will scoff at anyone suggesting social media is an oppressive force, smear us all as "reactionaries" or Luddites, and offer tepid suggestions to our corporate masters that they slightly lessen the harm the Feed does to teenage girls.

In this way, we can all pretend there is no real problem with the machine itself, only the mental fortitude of a handful of young women who really should know better. Just like any other symptom of the harm capitalism causes to humans, we'll pretend it's isolated, unrelated to the system itself, or due to some moral failing of its victims, all the while letting ourselves be ground by gears lubricated not with oil but with the blood and gore of crushed human meaning.

The Revolution of the Return Home

As I write this, I'm sipping coffee while staring out upon the bare branches of an oak just outside my kitchen. It's the day after Christmas: utterly quiet in the house now, quiet on the street outside, grey but not sullen. Peaceful. Really beautiful.

Yesterday, we hosted my sister and her two sons. There were supposed to be many more family members here, but some of them got a stomach virus and ended up in a hospital emergency room. Not quite what one hopes for on a holiday but, along with my partner and his mother, we six had a rather charming and warm afternoon. We enjoyed the exchange of gifts, a meal (I made lasagna, which has been the traditional holiday meal for my sisters and I since we were young), and a sense of continuity and especially of normal life despite the political and social chaos of the world.

The last few weeks I've been a bit out of sorts. I've written about this before, how there's a moment around each solar point of the year (the 8 holy days of the Celtic-pagan calendar) that feels a lot like just before you shift a gear on a bike. The force you use is no longer gripping the way it's needed, or it's gripping too hard. The solar point is the moment you need to shift.

The winter solstice is mid-winter in this reckoning. This makes more sense in the land where I live than the Roman calendar marking that date as the beginning of winter. At Samhain (1 November) the first extremely cold days started, and by Imbolc (2 February) the first sprouting of some hardier plants begins. The solstice is the mid-point between these.

So, I'm halfway through winter here.

Historically, in this land, this is when the final culling of herds would happen. The ancestral peoples here (up to only about 100 years ago) would slaughter the animals they would need to eat through the rest of the winter and into early spring. Now we just buy packaged meat from grocery stores, so we've forgotten this natural cycle. Regardless, it's still with us, preserved especially in the rituals of resolutions and reflection around New Year's Day and the very large dinners many people still cook on Christmas.

That "out of sorts" feeling I mentioned has been exactly that, the contemplation of what needs to hang about for the next full cycle of the year and what can and should be culled. We generally think of culling as a negative thing, an unfortunate necessity perhaps but otherwise worth avoiding. Predators are said to cull herds of the sick and old. Culling, though, is a lot more like pruning. Every gardener learns quickly that cutting away some branches and leaves actually helps the plant grow. Culling is the same, cutting back some parts so the larger part can continue.

It may be difficult to inhabit this knowledge but culling and pruning align more closely to what we see as political conservatism than to political liberalism. Conservatism urges the continuation of things by pulling some things back and sees, in endless growth and expansion, a recipe for starvation and death. Of course, that's not generally how conservatism maps onto political parties any longer—it's difficult to find truly conservative Republican politicians in the United States or truly conservative Tories in the United Kingdom.

If anything, this kind of conservatism maps more to Green or other environmentalist parties in Europe, though still not very closely. The kind of Green party politics that are often ridiculed and vilified by liberals and leftists, both in Europe and the United States, tend to be the most conservative. For instance, opposition to nuclear power production, genetically modified organisms, and 5G rollout derives from a conservative stance against capitalist expansion in directions that could lead to irreparable environmental and societal harm.

Such opposition is typically smeared as reactionary, anti-science, and superstitious by progressive politicians and thinkers. Leftists in the United States (particularly the Democratic Socialist left, centered around the journal Jacobin) ridicule this kind of conservatism. In this, they are much more in alignment with the capitalists of Silicon Valley and the corporate-sponsored politicians of both major US political parties.

This conservatism—hardly represented by any major political movement—is also seen in the populist reactions against digital vaccine passports and increased government restrictions of human movement and interaction in the name of public health. Though governments and public health officials introduce proposals and new regimes in the name of protecting the vulnerable and stopping the spread of a virus, there is always a larger concern few of them ever mention: the continuation of capitalist economic expansion.

Remember that there were other options to deal with the spread of COVID. A total shutdown of all economic exchange and international travel for a few months at the beginning of the outbreak—which is what quite a few public health officials and scientists urged—would have significantly slowed the transmission. Of course, this would have also completely emptied the treasuries of every government in the world since their citizens would only have agreed to such measures in return for a kind of emergency socialism the capitalists would never have been able to claw back.

The other option would have been to let the plague run its course. This would potentially have meant mass death, yes, but mass death doesn't mean the same thing to a capitalist that it means to us. For us, it's sad and terrible. For a capitalist, it means inflationary wages and labor shortages.

The last time a plague swept through the world, it destroyed feudalism. Landowners couldn't find enough serfs to work their land any longer, and those remaining serfs suddenly had significant power. The labor shortage this created is one of the primary reasons the ruling class resorted to colonial exploits and slave-taking, returning to "primitive accumulation" to save their position and re-assert dominance over the peasantry in Europe.

Neither options is really desirable. The point in mentioning them is to show that maintaining the current expansionary growth of capitalism has always been a primary (though obscured) motive in government policy decisions. Progress must continue at all costs, which means that labor availability and capitalist economic activity must not be damaged in any attempt to deal with the crisis this plague has caused. Forcing people to take vaccines created through capitalist production and distribution keeps the world headed towards more capitalism. Telling people to keep working, but from home, means the capitalists get to keep exploiting labor in new ways instead of redistributing their wealth back to those who created it for them.

Here you might be inclined to object, though: Isn't this also a kind of conservatism? Keeping the system in place rather than letting it undergo some revolutionary change through crisis—isn't this a kind of anti-progress stance? It would be, but only if we treat the present situation as if it has always been the situation. It hasn't. In fact, the current iteration of global capitalist exchange—in which industrial production for consumer goods is outsourced to China, container-shipped to every port in the world, and then distributed from central warehouses to store shelves or other warehouses where they are then sorted by Amazon or other companies to be shipped again direct to homes—is only a few decades old.

If you are in your 20s, your grandparents grew up in a world where "made in China" was a rarity and most things they ate were grown within a few hundred miles of their home. Sure, they couldn't get strawberries in winter or have anything they might want shipped with just one click, but they also lived in a world where a disease showing up halfway across the world would have taken more than a handful of months to ravage their neighbors.

Go back even further and, with the exception of the Spanish Flu, you don't see catastrophic diseases quickly sweeping across vast distances and through varied societies until the Black Death. And of course, the Spanish Flu only spread so widely because of a world war that caused soldiers from across the world to congregate in the same geographical locations to kill each other and then bring back illness to their families and homelands.

The Black Death in Europe was primarily spread across large geographical distances through merchant trade. The transmission of plague occurs so fast now because it uses the same transmission networks built to accommodate the new modes of capitalist industrial production and distribution, as well as the secondary consumption economies (business travel and tourism) for which airline networks have expanded. These networks are newly expanded in order to increase capitalist production and exchange, just as mercantile networks in the late Middle Ages expanded to increase the wealth of cities.

The problem here is expansion and the drive toward endless (and reckless) growth. That growth is liberal in the political and economic sense: laissez-faire, free trade, few restrictions, no boundaries, no borders, all things which capitalists require to continue. And with that expansion come costs, costs paid not by those who push for and profit from these policies but by those who never have any say in such matters.

Plague is one of those costs, and it is also a great moment of profit for some pharmaceutical companies, for online retailers like Amazon, and for other opportunists eager to seize on the societal disruption it has caused. It's also a perfect moment for governments needing to strengthen their position of dominance over their citizens, a moment to test the viability of social credit models and re-introduce tiered rights systems supposedly abolished by democracy. Most of all it's a perfect moment to change the moral order, to encourage the kind of social opprobrium directed at those who don't always wear their masks the right way or fear getting injected with something the government mandates.

All of this is done to make sure capitalism can keep expanding. Shutting down the international distribution and travel networks that the capitalists created would have significantly slowed the plague, likely giving local governments and emergency services the time to prepare. That would have been the conservative solution, by which I also mean a radical solution ("radical" means "root").

This radical solution would have caused a crisis the capitalists could not survive. It would have been a revolutionary act, the only kind of revolution that I find I believe in anymore. There are two leftist ideas about what a revolution is, one of which is shared by the kind of conservatism I mention. In the other, revolution is a turn toward progress, toward an expansion of technology, rights, new kinds of social arrangements, and new kinds of labor. When a Silicon Valley CEO calls something revolutionary, that's what he means. So do many of the people who think that smashing windows or embracing new identities is revolutionary. This is the sort of "revolutionizing" that *The Communist Manifesto* aligned with the bourgeoisie; the changing of all modes of production and therefore all social relations as well.

There is another kind of revolution, though, the one Walter Benjamin described:

> "Marx says that revolutions are the locomotives of world history. But the situation may be quite different. Perhaps revolutions are not the train ride, but the human race grabbing for the emergency brake."

This sort of revolution is ultimately a conservative one. It doesn't want to keep going, to keep expanding. It wants a rest, a pause, maybe even a complete turn away from the direction in which everything's been going. Instead of the promised smartphone in every pocket, it thinks maybe we could all just talk to each other in person again like we'd been doing for millennia. Instead of one-click shopping and global distribution of industrial production, maybe we could know the people who make things for us and not buy so much. Instead of remaking society and introducing new surveillance and tracking measures to keep capitalism going during a plague, maybe we could see this as a really good reason to pull the emergency brake on the train of progress.

This kind of revolution is conservative, but it does not map to what we think of as right or left. It has no directional orientation at all except toward home, the body, and the earth. It is the conservatism of a gardener who knows she must thin some plantings from a pot and prune some branches from a rosebush in order to have more flowers.

It's the conservatism of the villagers who decide which animals to cull so that both the herd and the humans who tend them will thrive. And it's the conservatism of "conservationism," a much older idea that, before environmentalism, sought to keep the forests and streams around so that people a hundred years on would get to meet them too.

So yes, I believe in revolution, but only this kind, the conservative sort. I'd like to see humans survive, and also the forests. I'd like people to keep being able to meet together without first needing to show a QR code, just like we've been doing for all our human existence. I'd like the grandchildren of my nephews to get to meet the descendants of the animals I encounter on my daily walks, rather than learn about them from extinction lists.

Revolution means to "turn again," but wheels don't only go in one direction. It's okay to turn back a bit, just as we might turn back on a path that we realize was leading the wrong way. Some people—who also stand to profit quite a bit from this—are telling us all to keep going, keep riding, that we'll eventually get to their promised land. They call that direction "forward," but circles don't really have a forward or a backward, nor an end nor a beginning. The direction we're going is completely relative to where we are standing.

So, yes, I guess I do still believe in revolution. Not the kind that wants to change the world, though, nor the kind that believes we're best marching endlessly toward a future someone else dreamed up for us. Instead, the only revolutionary—and the only revolution—that I trust is the one that looks around at its companions, surveys the distance, and says, in love, "Hey—I think we've gone far enough. Let's go home now."

Choosing To Be Violent

I.

Last night, after watching several videos of "smash-and-grab" burglaries, I heard a mouse scream. If you've never lived in the countryside, or never had a cat, perhaps you've never heard this scream. It's a really chilling sound, one that you never quite get used to. If you've not heard it, it may be difficult to imagine. One thinks of a mouse "squeaking," or perhaps chittering, or maybe not making any sound at all. In its death throes, though, a mouse's screams can be quite terrifying.

When a mouse screams, it sounds like a very young child. If the mouse is particularly close but not within sight, it's easy, for a moment, to mistake the sound for that of a girl being brutally and horrifically attacked.

That's the sound I heard at first last night. It was late, and because of the extreme heat here the window in my office was open. That window overlooks part of a stream, one of the few that still has any water in it around here. Because of that water and because of its dense and lush plant and tree cover, it's a bit of an oasis for all the animal life around here. Deer come to drink at it, as does a fox. There is a blue heron, and several white cranes I see there quite often, especially right after we've chased them away from our koi pond.

That's where the mouse died, screaming.

I suspect it was one of the owls who live in the large oak just behind our house. I hear them at night, very close. Occasionally their calls will echo through our house—because all our windows are open at night to deal with the heat of the day—in a way that makes them seem to be inside with us. Other birds actually do come inside, and they are not very easy to coax back out no matter how desperate they are to flee.

The owls never come inside, though. Sometimes a mouse does, more often before our cat died. Our cat would bring them in proudly, and sometimes they'd still be screaming. If they were already dead or at least immobile, we'd let her eat them in the house. When they were still screaming, still fighting, however, we'd instead rush to capture them and bring them outside.

Our cat was rarely happy about this, and I think she often felt betrayed. Our intention wasn't really to save the mouse (though if it fled and survived, we'd be fine with that outcome too), but rather to make sure it would not end up somewhere inside our walls. Occasionally she'd play with a mouse too much, wait too long for the *coup de grâce*, and consequentially it would escape and hide somewhere she couldn't get it.

Sadly, our cat is gone, and I don't think it was a neighbor's cat killing that mouse last night. I think it was the owl, though it's just as possible it was the fox. I'd heard the fox barking a few nights before, by the stream. I've never seen a fox kill a mouse (they're too crafty to let you witness them hunting), so I don't know if such kills are slow and loud or fast and quick. It was either a fox or an owl. Or maybe a cat. Regardless, something killed a mouse, and its screams filled my ear for a good 45 seconds before it finally went silent.

II.

Maybe eight years ago, around this time of year, and around the same time of night that I heard the mouse screaming, I was standing on the balcony of a house in Seattle. I had been writing and went outside to smoke a cigarette and think. Not far in the distance I heard a staccato sound repeat, first four times, then once more and then, after a pregnant pause, a final.

"Six," I said aloud to myself. I remember thinking it both odd and interesting that there was such a long pause between the fifth and sixth gunshot. The first four had been quick, fired in urgency. The fifth sounded a bit more thought-out, a shot of more even intention. But what was the shooter thinking between that fifth and sixth shot? What thoughts filled his head, what emotions ran through his body, and what logic swept through him to conclude that five shots were not enough? Was his victim still moving, twitching as the blood gushed from his body? Did the shooter want to make sure his victim was dead, or was that final shot just a statement? Or, because the people who will blow each other to pieces aren't really the most thoughtful sorts, maybe it was like drinking that last bit of an oversized soda he'd ordered. He wasn't thirsty anymore, but there was still some left, so why not empty it?

The sound of gunshots was rather common in that neighborhood. I lived for a time in the "Central District" of Seattle, a historically black neighborhood with intense poverty and a very, very high crime rate. Crack was everywhere, and muggings, and break-ins, and even that old-timey urban crime, "purse-snatching." I witnessed the latter quite often, and one time was even knocked to the ground by a thief fleeing his victim. I'd been too slow to notice what was happening, and he ran into me, and I fell, and then, thirty seconds later, the young woman the thief had stolen from was helping me up from the ground. She was crying, she'd broken a heel trying to run after him, her house keys and her phone were both in the stolen purse, and there was nothing I could do to console her.

I got so used to such events that they stopped feeling noteworthy. I say that, but that's not fully honest, because I remember that every time I'd witness such an incident, I'd actively try to narrate it away. I'd filter events like that shooting to make sure I didn't draw racist conclusions about it. Sure, there were a lot of people with one skin color shooting other people with the same skin color, just down the street, and every purse-snatching and burglary I'd witness or hear about was done by someone with that same skin color, but I'd remind myself of the institutional and systemic forces tying these events together. And anyway, people with that skin color were poorer and so had "more reason" to steal than others, so they were, in a way, justified in doing so, especially if their targets had more wealth than they did.

Listening to that mouse screaming last night, I finally understood how much of that mental filtering and re-narration I'd done while in the US, and how artificial it had all been. I was trying to make sure I never became a "racist," but there was never actually any risk of that. I didn't think then, nor do I think now, nor will I ever think that people with one skin color are inherently anything that people with another skin color are not.

Why the re-narration, then? Why filter every event through an ideological frame that minimized guilt and offered justification for absurd violence? Why tell myself that the woman who'd been robbed was somehow not really a victim because of her skin color, while the man who'd robbed her was not really a victimizer because of his?

III.

Judging by its screams, the mouse outside my window last night died a really violent death. The man that shooter murdered 8 years ago near my house also died a really violent death. Humans kill other humans, and they kill animals. Animals kill other animals. This is how it is, how it always has been, how it always will be. But things go awry when we try to assign meaning and justification to violence, to develop moral frameworks about when violence is not "really" violence. Such frameworks can only ever apply to humans, and they always come down to ideological sympathies—whether or not we can imagine ourselves doing such violence also.

Was the owl (or possibly a fox) "justified" in its violence against the mouse? This is the wrong question, of course, because justice and justification are human constructions. We might feel bad for the mouse, but we understand that our sympathy for it is irrelevant to its existence as a mouse and the owl's existence as an owl. We are neither mice nor owls, and no matter what preference we might have for one or the other, any application of morality to their interactions would be ridiculous.

When violence involves humans, though—well, we're also human. And because we're human, we use imagination and empathy to figure out whether we'd behave the same way, given the same circumstances.

IV.

I heard the mouse scream after watching several videos of "smash and grab" burglaries. I find these events rather fascinating, especially because their occurrence seems to be increasing rapidly in the

United States and has become a raw field of propaganda for both the far right and the anarchist left there. In such burglaries, a group of people—sometimes up to a hundred or so—swarm a business, a mall, or sometimes even a vehicle stopped at a traffic light. They force entry and quickly take everything that is visible and valuable before absconding just as quickly from the scene, often scattering in multiple directions so that police cannot capture everyone.

Such events aren't unique to the United States, nor are they new. They're a type of brigandism, a common form of "highway robbery" in which a group of men would swarm a traveling merchant or peasant caravan and steal everything they could carry away. In fact, this is one of the oldest forms of what Marx called "primitive accumulation," the direct taking of wealth by violent and extra-economic means. Brigandism is called piracy when it happens on the water rather than on land and is, technically, what vikings did.

What particularly fascinates me about these events are the political narratives that spring up around them, re-storying them either as a sign of the sudden collapse of civilization and order (the far-right narrative) or as a people's movement to take back wealth that was stolen from them (the American anarchist narrative). Both are baseless: There's nothing either new or politically conscious happening here. At best it's just the lumpenproletariat looking for a quick way to profit, and while some of the incidents are certainly spectacular, the amount of stolen wealth they involve is a drop in the ocean compared to the British Museum's antiquities collection.

When I first saw videos of these burglaries—right about the time I heard those gunshots from that Seattle balcony—I recall feeling a kind of glee for the perpetrators and a complete callousness towards the businesses. While I'm not embarrassed by my memory of that reaction, I am curious about it. The mouse's scream made me wonder why I'd felt that way. That feeling, I now understand, came from the same place as my re-narration of street crime and shootings. I'd merely switched the polarity between victim and perpetrator, convincing myself that the owners of the shops "deserved" the event and those that robbed them were affecting political justice. That is of course what anarchists do now: overlaying their own ideological goals and coordinates on apolitical events.

I still find these events fascinating, and the reason is precisely because they're not new. They re-historicize our modern present or, to borrow from Dipesh Chakrabarty, they "provincialize" our supposedly post-historical age. Such brigandism is exactly how the initial wealth of the capitalists was acquired, wealth which they then institutionalized as capital. Smash-and-grab burglaries are just people trying to do the same thing, despite whatever justifications and narratives they—or we—might try to overlay upon them.

Would I join a group of people to go rob a mall or smash in the windows of a stopped SUV? Nah, because that just sounds like an awful thing to do. Would I shoot up another person because he owed me money for the crack I gave him to sell for me? No, unless I was addicted to crack also. Then maybe I would, but of course it would take an epic transformation in my personality to get to the point where I'd even consider smoking crack. Would I run past a woman and steal the purse off her shoulder? Gods no, nor can I imagine the kind of mindset I'd require to consider that an idea worth entertaining.

Maybe, maybe, decades and centuries of "institutionalized" and "systemic" racism might have been able to create a version of me that would do such a thing. Maybe generations of despair and hopelessness might lead me to such a point. But there would have to be one more crucial element: Hatred.

You need to actually hate someone in order to do something willfully violent to them. That hatred need not be of the enraged sort, however. Hatred can also be the cold dehumanization that turns people into objects rather than connected beings. Both kinds of hatred, together, are necessary to enact genocide and war, but they're also required for more singular crimes.

To kill someone with a gun, or to rob them, or to rape them, you have to hate them. They have to be not-human to you, and there are plenty of ways to get to that point. You can decide that they have hurt you in some way, and you are therefore justified in harming them, as with the narcissistic and psychopathic sorts who create stories in which they are eternal victims. You can decide they're part of some larger "system" that harmed you or "keeps you down," meaning their bodies and belongings are fair game for pillaging. Similarly, you can decide they are non-human because of some fantasy about race, in either direction. Or you can just see them as objects, filtering out and narrating away any proof of their humanity.

VI.

This doesn't happen anywhere else in nature. The owl doesn't need to "dehumanize" the mouse, or even to "demousify" it. It's a mouse, and owls eat mice (among other things), and that's all. There's an order to it, and it's one that humans haven't imposed, cannot alter, and probably cannot fully understand. All we can understand is the human, and the human is a right mess. If there's an order to human violence, it's a terrifying order, and probably also unalterable. I think the most we can do is to re-assert what's probably the only unique thing about humans: Choice.

The owl doesn't choose to be violent. It just is violent, and other things as well. Humans are likewise violent and many other things, but the difference is that we have some say in enacting violence. We can choose to rape or not to rape, to shoot someone or not to shoot someone, to rob a woman on the street or not to rob her. Most of us—the overwhelming majority of us on earth—choose not to.

Those who enact violence have chosen to do so. Sure, there might be all sorts of justifications that the perpetrators come up with or that the witnesses narrate in to explain why that choice seemed like a good one, or like the "only" option. The thing is, that's all just ideological masturbation, mental contortions we go through because we like things nice and tidy in our minds. We like to have reasons for violence, external and traceable causes for it. We don't like to admit that humans are inherently violent, even though we are happy to believe we're inherently other things.

One problem with this denial is that our inherent violence is what makes the choice not to be violent so beautiful. Just as our inherent kindness is what makes being unkind or malicious so tragic. Our inherent rampant sexual desire makes the choice to commit to one person so powerful, and our inherent reflex for care and nurturing is what makes our abandonment of any person in need so sorrowful.

The Most Terrible Secret

Perhaps the most terrible secret I have ever learned is that we are solely and fully responsible for our own joy. This may sound like "white light" bullshit, especially if you consider yourself a radical or a leftist. The "White Light" movement—or "white light spirituality"—stems from a philosophy popular in the 1800s called New Thought. You already know New Thought if you've ever encountered the phrase "mind over matter," or "law of attraction," or the idea that thinking positive thoughts makes your life better.

Much of New Age spirituality—all the ideas about raising your consciousness or "vibration" to improve your own life and the lives of others around you—descends from this school of thought, as well as the faith healing (including Mary Baker Eddy's Christian Science) that ran rampant throughout the United States in the nineteenth and twentieth centuries. All these philosophies teach basically the same thing: that most of the shitty circumstances in life can be changed through application of mental discipline or a shift of thought patterns. This includes physical conditions such as illness and poverty, as well as social problems like relationship issues, loneliness, depression, and alienation.

And most of it is bullshit, but unfortunately most of it is also true.

There is a school of psychotherapy—the one that I've seen deliver the most profound effects for many of my friends who've used it—called Cognitive Behavioral Therapy. Unlike more traditional approaches (that often involve pharmaceuticals), CBT attempts to identify the core beliefs underlying destructive or unhealthy patterns in someone's life, and then guide them into a place where they can change those beliefs.

For instance, consider a person who is constantly depressed and has had a long series of failed relationships. The therapist using CBT would attempt to discover what that person thinks about themself and how they narrate those relationships. The therapist would then try to tease out the core beliefs that might be leading the person to sabotage themself and their relationships. Once those are identified, the therapist would suggest new beliefs and thought patterns that might help the person become less depressed and have more success in relationships.

The key question constantly posed to a patient in Cognitive Behavioral Therapy is some form of, "Have you tried thinking a different way about this?" A person who, for example, believes that they will never have healthy relationships because of past abuse would be encouraged to question this belief, possibly by questioning the relationship between that abuse and the way they define themselves. Perhaps the person believes that, in some way, they deserved the abuse, or that they can never heal from that pain, or that they are still being abused even when they are not. Those beliefs prevent them from having healthier relationships, and thus need to be replaced with more useful beliefs.

By this point, I've likely triggered an emotional reaction in some of you reading this, because my description of this scenario seems to "victim blame," to put the onus for all those situations on the suffering person, rather than on the person who caused the suffering in the first place. Please feel free to sit with that emotion, because that's exactly the kind of reaction I used to have to such narratives, too. Especially if you're a leftist, the very idea that a person's suffering might be more strongly linked to their thought patterns than to external circumstances is reminiscent of the core belief of capitalism: "If you're poor, it's your own fault."

But "if you're poor, it's your own fault" is also a core belief that a therapist using Cognitive Behavioral Therapy might try to tease out and help a person change. The key here is the word "fault," which belongs to a mental framework in which wealth and poverty are signifiers of a moral order. Put another way, "if you're poor it's your fault" signals a belief that wealth is tied to morality. The more moral you are, the more wealth you will have; the less moral you are, the poorer you will be.

The inverse—what Nietzsche called "slave morality"—is also a false belief: The wealthy are immoral, the poor are righteous. This, of course, forms the basis of a lot of current leftist thought, especially in the United States, and is ultimately as self-defeating a belief system as the one it attempts to fight. Poverty and wealth are material conditions, not moral positions. There is no Judeo-Christian mono-god distributing wealth to his elect, nor is there a social justice version of that god recording the suffering of the poor in moral ledgers from which they can later draw social capital.

While Marx showed that the conditions of the poor are orchestrated by those who have already accumulated financial wealth, the whole point of *The Communist Manifesto*, and the rest of his works, was that the working classes could significantly better their conditions by reaching a mental state called "class consciousness." There is no moral fault or blame to be ascribed to the capitalists, nor to the working classes, only a social arrangement that can be changed if the workers want it badly enough.

That is to say, New Thought and white light spirituality have something in common with the core materialist assertion of Marxism. Contrast this with Critical Race Theory and the narcissism of social justice identity politics. These latter frameworks are moral ones, assigning blame and fault to an apex-oppressor class (white cis-het-abled men) who possess an ineffable yet omnipotent, morally evil force called "privilege." The rest of the world, the "good" people, are relentless and eternal victims, unable to ever attain happiness, joy, or even a stable existence because of esoteric and occulted forces like "white supremacy" and "cis-hetero-patriarchy."

I once thought these things too. I also thought things like "I'll always be poor because of capitalism," and "I will never be treated as an equal in a relationship." It turns out these were tendrils of more deeply rooted core beliefs, especially "I have no power over my own life," "I don't deserve better," and "my suffering makes me morally righteous."

These beliefs manifested in ways that I now find fascinating but that initially—when I first learned to explore them—embarrassed the hell out of me. For instance, whenever I would meet someone who seemed to be healthier, happier, and wealthier than I did, I assumed they were amoral, or that they had done something immoral to achieve that condition. How could they possibly enjoy life when there is so much suffering in the world? How could they afford to eat healthy food, go to the doctor, get their teeth fixed, buy new clothes, without deadening their souls?

Their "secret" was embarrassingly simple and terrible: *They merely let themselves.* An opportunity appeared in front of them and they pursued it, rather than telling themselves it "wasn't for them." They saw how they wanted to live and then lived that way, without endlessly debating whether they "deserved" such a life. They pursued relationships that reflected the kind of love they wanted to both give and receive, rather than settling for the first unstable, broken person who showed unhinged interest in them. And they left relationships that didn't bring joy or reciprocate the effort, attention, and care they offered.

For such people, there's no "secret" to living this way. Doing so is quite obvious to them. Once I figured it out, too, it's the most gods-damned self-evident thing. The "secret" is not postponing your life, and no longer holding yourself hostage to ideologies or moral frameworks that assign value and fault to suffering or joy.

The most terrible part of all this, for me, is the "secret" of wealth. My income has barely changed over the last six years, yet there's so much wealth in my life that I feel absurdly rich. Wealth isn't money, and poverty is not the lack of money. Wealth comes from the earth, our relationship to it and to our bodies, not from dollar signs and paychecks. Wealth is the friends and relationships in your life, the air you breathe, the life that moves around and through you. It's not something anyone "deserves," but something anyone can recognize in their own life.

The financially rich are often just as miserable as the poor. I now personally know more millionaires than I ever thought possible, and most of them don't get to enjoy any of it. That's the other terrible part of this "secret:" those feelings of lack and want never go away, no matter how much you have, unless you learn to enjoy what is already around and inside you. To let yourself feel joy: That terrible secret both the poor and the rich can learn if they allow themselves.

Joy as Anti-Politics

Others have tried to write a framework for a "politics of joy," with absolutely depressing results. Such efforts will invariably fail because joy is one of the few human experiences that has successfully resisted politicization. Joy is neither left-wing nor right-wing, and no politics can ever create joy. The goal of modern politics and activism—just like the goal of consumer advertising—is to inculcate, harness, and re-channel mass disaffection, despair, and the feeling of lack and insufficiency in service to the goals of the few.

To do this, they must convince us that we are not responsible for our own joy, that something or someone outside ourselves is standing in the way of our fulfillment. It doesn't matter whether that external obstacle is an identity group (Muslims, men, the rich) or an intangible system (white supremacy, immigration, patriarchy, capitalism, communism), nations—and monotheism—conjure external enemies and future rewards to compel the masses towards violence.

Politics is ultimately anti-joy. People in joy lack nothing and therefore want nothing. Their desires are fulfilled, at least while they are in joy, because joy fulfills its own desire. You can be starving, or in prison, or on your deathbed and still feel joy. It is a particular orientation toward experience, not a result of experience. As such, it's ultimately the opposite of (and only cure for) *ressentiment. Ressentiment* says, "I cannot feel joy and therefore no one should." It actively prevents and walls out experiences of joy, and to do so it must choke the joy out of others.

Consider the bitter, childless old woman who sneers at the laughter of playing children, demanding curfews and laws to quiet them. She is in *ressentiment*. She is someone who has refused joy—not because she had no children, but because she made having children a condition of her joy. The angry man who shoots his former co-workers when he is laid off is likewise in *ressentiment*, because he made having that job the condition of his joy. The non-binary asexual who demands all displays of gay male kink sexuality be purged from Pride festivals, and the person who demands mass language changes ("chest feeding" rather than "breast feeding," or the elimination of all potential triggers from the public speech of strangers) are likewise in a state of *ressentiment*.

Ressentiment is reductive. It must reduce the experience of others to the joyless state of the person in *ressentiment*. Joy, on the other hand, is expansive. It is contagious, like the laughter of a child. It wants to share, to bring others into the experience. When we see the moon rise full and rose-gold over a hill, or see a rainbow, our first instinct is to call to all those within hearing distance to share our wonder.

"Join me," joy says, leaping from our hearts.

"Suffer as I suffer," *ressentiment* scowls, withering our souls.

Joy has no external source, and it is not based on circumstances. Joy does, however, lead you to change circumstances, to pursue situations in which that joy flows more easily, to stop striving for results that will not give you joy. There is no joy in striving against capitalism, but neither is there joy in striving for capitalist ends. Instead, there is joy in the raw life that capitalism, politics, and the state obscure—the human moments, the moments of being human in —and as—nature.

I took a brief pause while writing this to ride my bike to a store. My path led me through a forest divided by a road, and while riding home, the sun warming my skin erotically, the scent of the forest filling my nostrils and mind, I forgot myself completely, forgot this essay, forgot all of it and just was. A fawn crossed my path, regarding me calmly, unstartled. I laughed and said hello, then continued my ride home.

That is the joy of raw life, a joy which led me to live where I am, to give more time to the nature around me and to give myself more time to be in nature and so to be in joy. In such moments, I need nothing. I lack nothing. I just am. So, I fill my life with more such moments, cultivating them like one cultivates a garden. There is nothing political in these moments of joy. The most that modern politics can do is prevent them: paving over forests, putting up fences, making it illegal to be in among the trees. Even if a politics of joy were possible, it couldn't make joy happen.

What leads us to joy are our other experiences of joy. With each moment of joy, we learn to look toward more joy, to turn more often toward the horizon as the sun sets or the moon rises. We learn to cultivate friendships where joy is a mutual goal (and yes, to let die friendships where joy suffocates in the void of *ressentiment*). We learn to change our very way of seeing the world, to exorcise from our hearts all the beliefs that choke out our joy. We stop preventing, sabotaging, and prohibiting ourselves, just as we stop preventing, sabotaging, and prohibiting the pursuit of joy by others.

We learn to let ourselves be in joy. We learn to manifest joy. And the terrible secret becomes the most beautiful secret: We are the only ones who can do so.

The Poetic Mind

Perhaps one of the greatest shifts in collective human consciousness—affecting our social, moral, and political development—was the transition from oral to written language. That statement may sound mythic, perhaps incomprehensible, but you and I are communicating right now through written language, and so we start with a terrible disability. Every word I write, and every word you read, is immediately and historically limited in its meaning. These words are caged into static forms from which they cannot easily escape.

All words began as sounds in the throat of a human. The earliest ones are thought to have been attempts at mimicry, a kind of childlike play between our ancestors and the world around them. Consider how the rush of wind through the trees makes a sound that we can hear and recognize. That sound—which we humans can approximate by funneling directed breath through our lips and shaping its undulation with our tongues—may have formed the precursor of the sounds we signify with the letters "h" and "sh" in English. The staccato chirp of birds, heard everywhere by our ancestors whether in forest or field, is still approximated by what phoneticians call affricates ("ch" in English, for example, thus "chirp.")

The sounds of nature, composing what can fairly be called a relentless symphony, are not just background noise. The crackle of fire and the rush of water, the rumble of thunder across the sky and the howl of a wolf, all have meaning. That meaning exists both at the level of denotation (what it signifies) and connotation (the context of the sound related to the hearer). The "snap" of a twig is the denotation, meaning that a twig has snapped, but the sound itself does not convey to us the connotation, that is whether it was a nearby deer or a wolf who caused that twig to snap.

Language was likely born from the process of humans learning to interpret the sounds around them, to draw relevancy and meaning from them, and to repeat them to others. Just as the sounds made by a mother to an infant sound foreign and incomprehensible at first, and later take on clearly codified symbolism, those who came before us encountered a world of noisy senselessness and soon found within that noise an endless world of meaning.

The development of language did not rely only on our ears, however. Our eyes and skin are always telling us things as well. Gestures are pregnant with meaning, whether it be a hug, a hand wave, a slap, a pointed finger, or a solid stare. So too the vision of a stag standing in a forest, or a mammoth or aurochs walking away from or rushing toward us.

Our earliest attempts to make that meaning static were images, paintings of animals on the walls of caves and likely elsewhere (though these unprotected paintings did not survive the weathering effects of time). Indigenous peoples with mostly uninterrupted oral traditions often speak of animals and plants as their teachers or even their ancestors, and it is not difficult to see the truth in this. A flock of geese flying south is a thing of deep beauty and inspires a moment of awe, but it is also a warning that the snows and freezes are coming. A great elk tearing furiously through bramble is a sight, and sound, that also speaks of the predator chasing him. The dog who has deigned to live alongside humans speaks medicine and wisdom when he turns his nose up and refuses to eat an animal those humans have just killed, and they would do well to heed him.

Language is ancient, but writing is much more recent. We started out with pictures, images, often clumsy yet efficient lines mimicking the shapes of things in nature. Debates rage about how civilization started, whether it began with the birth of agriculture or the birth of cities. Writing is rarely if ever named as the culprit, despite the fact that writing arose just a little bit before cities did, in our historical record.

The very first shift from pictographs (signs directly representing a thing) to cuneiform, logograms, and hieroglyphs (signs representing a part of a thing, or a quantity, or the general idea of a thing) began 5,500 years ago. Our writing is now a deeply abstracted form, far removed from these earlier attempts at representation. Each word of this essay is formed from a combination of a set of 26 symbols signifying an esoteric pattern of sounds that form words. That symbol set—our phonetic alphabet—preserves very little of the ancient symbolic roots of our early attempts to write. Unlike Norse runes—which were also phonetic yet bore sacred meanings in and of themselves—our letters are fully disconnected from the natural world and symbolize nothing but sound.

So, it's incredibly easy for us to forget—if we ever knew—that language was once related to the world around us. We can imagine that we speak the world into existence, shaping our universe through our mastery of symbol sets. This is the most limiting legacy of the religions "of the book," whose singular god is written to have simply said, "Let there be light," and it became so.

Words pinned the natural world into symbol, yet the Western legacy and all its destructive industry is the manifestation of the "word made flesh." We speak ideas and they rule the world, initiating wars and holocausts, political struggle and self-annihilation, marching unhesitatingly, without even a comma's-worth of pause, toward the written language's final period.

The first transition from pictograph to cuneiform, in Mesopotamia, was necessitated by accounting. A clay tablet could show you the image of a goat or a bushel of wheat, but it is inefficient to draw a hundred such images when you could just add a few more scratches to symbolize "you owe me this many." The nature of that transition tied writing to wealth and the lack thereof, and so it was the earliest scribes who held the power, within their styluses, over the destinies of men.

The power of the writer has not changed since that time, though there are many more of us. With the stroke of a pen—or more often now the stroke of a key—a bureaucrat or even a mere office clerk can foreclose on your house, turn off your electricity, cause a road to be built through a forest, or confine millions to their homes. A policy is written, and so water is poisoned, or a war is started. A book of theory is scribed and suddenly our ideas about ourselves change completely.

Mastery of the written word has come to trump mastery of any other skill humans have learned and cherished, yet mastery of the spoken word persists just beyond it. Powerful propaganda cannot exist without the propagandist's understanding of how we hear words in our heads, how their meanings unfold within the alembics of individual consciousness. Consider double-speak and dog-whistles, two terms we use to describe the manipulation of meaning within the orally-constructed consciousness of the hearer. A politician can say two things at the same time, and like the twig snap in the forest his meaning depends entirely on subjective context.

In recent memory, the most famous of these examples is perhaps Donald Trump's recorded statement, "grab her by the pussy," which enraged liberals while conservatives shrugged and wondered why the liberals were so upset. Both sides heard the same words in very different contexts. Liberals heard a man speaking about sexually assaulting a woman, while conservatives heard the feminization of a popular lower-class phrase derived from sales lingo, "Grab him by the balls."

Such mastery is essential to the successful wielding of political power within democracies. You must convince your supporters that you are speaking to their contexts, while veiling your meaning enough to confound those who oppose such contexts.. Thus Obama could convince so many on each side that he represented real political "change," drawing both progressives and conservatives into social struggle against each other while he altered nothing about the US imperialist and capitalist system. Thus George W. Bush could speak of bombing people to bring them freedom and democracy while his opponents outdid themselves trying to prove to his supporters that they were also for freedom and democracy. Thus Bill Clinton could famously argue before the public, "It depends on what the meaning of the word 'is' is. If 'is' means is and never has been, that is not—that is one thing."

To rule, you must know something about words that only poets understand. Words rarely if ever mean just one thing. They are abstractions of things themselves, shoddy constructions that cannot hold, as T.S. Eliot says:

> Words strain,
> Crack and sometimes break, under the burden,
> Under the tension, slip, slide, perish,
> Decay with imprecision, will not stay in place,
> Will not stay still.

Words are used to obscure meaning as often as to reveal it, and the key to knowing the difference is remembering their original relationship to the natural world. The further a word is removed from that original relationship, the more obfuscated its meaning becomes, until only the initiated can understand it. This is the purpose of lingo and jargon, specialized language meant to occult what is being said to those who don't already subscribe to the social and epistemological codes producing such speech. The legalese of consent forms and contracts obscures meaning from those over which such documents have power, while the contorted strings of ill-defined concepts in academic texts wall out the unwashed masses who might otherwise challenge their meaning.

Consider the infamous passage that won the inaugural award of the yearly "Bad Writing Contest" by Judith Butler:

> The move from the structuralist account in which capital is understood to structure social relations in relatively homologous ways to a view of hegemony in which power relations are subject to repetition, convergence, and rearticulation brought the question of temporality into the thinking of structure, and marked a shift from a form of Althusserian theory that takes structural totalities as theoretical objects to one in which the insights into the contingent possibility of structure inaugurate a renewed conception of hegemony as bound up with the contingent sites and strategies of the rearticulation of power.

Such writing is only possible when speaking of ideas fully abstracted from the world of the Real. Something is being communicated, in such passages, but not to the masses. And regardless of the obscurity of this kind of writing—or perhaps because of that obscurity—it wields significant power to shape the world and manifest new realities.

"The word was made flesh, and dwelt among us" was said of the Christ, and is this not also the arcane art for which renaissance magicians strove and for which cloistered academics struggle? To claim power over the word is to claim power over the world, shifting the "structures" of consciousness to make manifest the visions of an elite few. Whether we like those elites or fear them, their power is undeniable and almost inescapable.

Almost inescapable, but not quite. Plato consigned poets to death in his utopian fantasies for the same reason bookstores consign their works to dusty, unmarked corners. The power of the poet is the power of death, which is also the province of the mystic, the witch living beyond the hedge, and the fool in the royal court. The poet's power is the power of negation, the magic of disenchantment. The poet knows words are also not-words, holding meaning and without meaning all at the same time. Words, for the poet, are as colors and shadows for the painter, not merely tools but also substances with which worlds can be depicted or destroyed.

The poet knows that the word is never only the word. Words have meaning, but meanings mean many things, dance together, conflict, war against each other like divine lovers. The poet knows this dance, knows this war, knows this love, and teaches us to know this too. Only in the poet's mind can the multiple and opposite truths of a statement be held simultaneously because the poet listens not just to words but also to their echoes. To be a poet you must live in the minds of others as well as in your own. You must hear what they hear and understand why they hear it.

This is the nature of the poetic mind, the mind that first translated the meaning of bird song and wolf howl into the realm of human understanding. The wolf speaks for itself, but its voice conveys other meanings to those who hear it. The bird is not singing to us, yet in its song is wisdom we can learn to decipher. The world is always singing, chanting, speaking, arguing, discussing, and most of all meaning, but the meaning we find will always and only be in translation.

Machines speak literally in binaries, in ons and offs. It is no wonder then that we humans—who speak through and with machines—have privileged literalism over mythic and poetic meaning. Words in a binary world can only have one meaning, symbols can only link once to the things they symbolize. There is only one thing that was "truly meant," just as there is only one way you should "truly feel."

We now have left or right to choose from, as we have the truth or "fake news." To the poetic mind, however, it's all both fake and true, just as a human has both a left and a right hand. It is not that truth is relative but that we are relative, or rather that we are constantly relating, clumsy translators of a world of voiced meaning spoken in languages we can never fully learn.

What the poet teaches is to hear the world and its words as they do. The shock of a poem is never in its content, but rather in the processes it unlocks in the mind of its audience. The poet plays with words, and juggles their meanings like a carnival actor, but it is all spectacle. The real prestige is that we do not notice, until the show is over, that the magician-thief slipped into the the cluttered storehouses of our minds and stole away our certainty that we can understand the world.

To read poetry—and better yet to hear it—is to let the mind again be opened. It is to hear not just as others hear but also how we hear ourselves. It is to hear, beyond all the poets' words and our own, how the world itself has always been speaking in sounds and with voices our words can never close in or capture.

The Unquiet Dead

My grandmother died a few days ago. I knew before my sister told me, though I didn't know that I knew. After I spoke with my sister, my partner pointed something out. For the last few weeks we've been remodeling several rooms in our home, including my office and a storage room. We were sorting things that we'd displaced into the garage, as we finished up the various construction projects, when I suddenly became distant, cold, and listless.

I begged off the last of the work and went upstairs. I thought I was just tired, or maybe beginning to get ill. It was the same sort of feeling I have during certain moons, a sense of sinking, like sitting in a draining tub. Then my sister texted me, asking if I had time to chat. When I saw that text, I knew what she would tell me.

One of the traditions we've mostly lost, in modern society, is that of ancestor veneration. Especially in the United States—where very few people live where their grandparents lived—and especially because of capitalism—compelling most to move long distances in search of work or survivable situations— displacement and rootlessness have become the default of human existence.

One might suppose that ancestors don't matter to us, though we spend millions on therapy to resolve unhelpful subconscious patterns and beliefs instilled in us by family members. We tell our therapists that our parents "messed us up," and our therapists help us understand how our parents got messed up themselves, and how we learned the wrong lessons from moments that were never meant to be instructive.

Cultures that engaged in ancestral veneration understood this as well. *Veneration* means "worship" in Latin, yes, but the word has older roots that manifest more obviously in other languages and refer to desire and a sense of striving after (venereal, as in *venereal* disease, preserves this sense of "desire"). Ancestors were people to strive after, to desire to become. And that's only half the story.

We can see the other half in Catholic ancestral rites, which are even less thinly veiled pagan continuations than saint veneration. At any Catholic church, family members can pay for a mass to be performed in the name of a dead relative. The official, theological reason for these masses is to speed the dead soul's transition from purgatory to paradise, and many masses are often performed for people who were particularly sinful during their lives.

This practice echoes pagan Roman rites of passage for the dead, as well as many of the funereal rites of the Germanic and Celtic peoples. These elaborate ceremonies were performed to help the dead "pass on," to keep peace between the dead and the living, and especially to prevent the unquiet dead from messing up the lives of those who remained.

African animist cultures had similar beliefs, and many Shinto, Hindu, and Buddhist beliefs reflect this concern about the unquiet dead as well. The unquiet dead continued to meddle in the lives of those who remained, their concerns and desires haunting the living such that they might as well not have died at all. The dead left unresolved things with the living, who were compelled to find a way to resolve them. So, the rites to speed their passage or pacify their souls, such as the Catholic masses for the dead, were also for the living. They were ritualistic methods of reconciling the lives of the dead with the lives of those who remained, a kind of communal act of resolution therapy.

This isn't to say that modern therapy is useless. On the contrary, without communal rituals of ancestral reconciliation, it's usually our only option, and a good one in their absence. However, this older kind of ritual is still possible and quite powerful.

Since my grandmother's death, I've begun to sort out her legacy in my own life. Of all my ancestors, she's been the most difficult to reconcile, because that legacy was both profoundly helpful and profoundly hurtful. Through her, I'm related to a famous 19th-century Supreme Court judge, and a famous poet, and also to Alfred Hitchcock. My Welsh ancestry comes through her as well. More interesting to me, however, is what I learned from her.

I think, more than anything else, I owe my intelligence to her. When I was young, living in squalor and miserable poverty, she would send me mass-market children's workbooks. You used to be able to buy these next to cash registers in grocery stores, workbooks full of math problems to solve, as well as grammar, history, science, and my favorite—atlases. Every few months she'd send a stack of these to me, her prepubescent grandson, and I'd finish all the problems and read through all the lessons and eagerly await her next gift.

I learned many positive things because of her, some of them very subtle arts which have proven to be boons in my life. Unfortunately, from her I first learned to feel shame about my body and sexuality and, particularly, my masculinity. I understand how this happened, how her own life required the suppression and obscuration of the sexuality of others. She was abused as a child, and her children were abused by the same person who abused her. She kept silent because it was too terrible to speak about, repressed everything about herself and urged everyone else to repress themselves too.

People who repress like that, who are nevertheless generous and kind in the rest of their relations, set up an unfortunate dynamic with those who love them. I adored my grandmother, and always wanted to impress her. And it was awful, because who I was and what I was doing would have shocked her, so I had to pretend to be otherwise.

The evening she died, I recounted a story to my husband about the great lengths to which I went to "keep up appearances" for her. It's quite hilarious, actually, so I'll tell you, too.

When I was 19, I lost my scholarship to the Christian college I attended because I admitted that I was gay. I knew this would disappoint her no end. She always told me I was the "smartest" of her grandchildren, and she was certain I would be a famous writer one day. My leaving university—and for being a homosexual, no less—would have really upset her.

So, I lied about why I left. I told her that I transferred to a better writing program at a different university. What I was really doing was taking a lot of LSD and smoking a lot of marijuana while working at an adult video store. Which may sound rather pathetic but it wasn't a bad life. I had quite a few really good friends, some of whom would hang out with me at work, waiting for me to close the store so we could hit a club and go dancing.

One of my friends, Jess, had taken a year off from Duke. She was my most "educated" friend, so it was she whom I asked, in a panic, if she'd pretend to be my girlfriend. My grandmother was coming to visit, and I was terrified. She wanted to see my university, and she wanted to meet my girlfriend. I never told her I had a girlfriend, only that I was dating someone. I didn't tell her that someone was a man.

Jess agreed—she actually thought it would be fun—so she waited with me at my apartment for my grandparents. I was worried about my grandmother seeing my apartment, because it was just part of an attic in an ancient six-story brownstone. I lucked out, though, because they couldn't find parking, so we had to meet them elsewhere.

Somewhere in one of my grandmothers' many photo albums is a picture of me standing next to a large sign. That's the entrance to the University of Southern Maine, where my grandmother believed I was going. I didn't even know where the university was until that day. Fortunately, Jess did, and she directed my grandfather from the back seat of the car. Posing in front of that sign while actual students walked by felt really awkward, but worse was to come.

See, I'd told my grandmother I was working at a video rental store as well as going to university. Now, she wanted to see my workplace, too, and in a panic I'd told her I was working at the largest one in the city, which was also a CD store and a cafe where all the most interesting people hung out. Suddenly, we were driving there.

Jess met my panicked look with her own, realizing what was about to happen. I was going to have to enter one of the coolest places in the city and pretend I worked there, while she and I tried to distract my grandmother from asking any of my supposed co-workers about me.

We were two blocks away when suddenly Jess started searching her purse. It was impossible to talk to each other without my grandparents overhearing, so I held my breath. Then, Jess pulled something triumphantly out of her purse, waved it at me quickly, and handed it to my grandmother.

It was a photograph. Me, smiling ridiculously, wearing the cheap polyester polo shirt that was part of my uniform. "It's a photo of him at work!" Jess said as she presented it to my grandmother.

Jess read the situation better than I had. My grandfather had become impatient with all the side trips and was not much for knowing the private details of all his grandchildren's lives anyway. He was more practical, down to earth. He'd grown up in a poor farming family in the Midwest and never really embraced all that East Coast obsession with status.

"Oh! That's great, Jess, thank you!" my grandmother said, staring at the photo while searching her own purse for her glasses.

My grandfather was happy, too. "I don't think I'll find parking, let's visit his store another day."

Jess smiled at me triumphantly. She was the best fake girlfriend a gay dude could ever have, and she proved it a moment later.

My grandmother asked if she could keep the photo, hold on to it forever as a memory of my life there. Jess asked if she could see it again for a moment, and my grandmother handed it back to her. Jess looked as if she were about to explode in laughter and shook her head.

"Do you mind if I just check to see if I still have the negatives? It's my favorite picture of him but if I have them, I can have a duplicate made and send it to you."

My grandmother absolutely saw the logic in this, and for years she told me that Jess was the perfect woman for me. My grandmother kept asking about her long after I told her that Jess had gone back to Duke. Sadly, I lost contact with Jess myself, though I hope perhaps someday she'll read this, and maybe she'll still have that photo.

I did so much to keep up appearances for my grandmother. Now that she is dead, I'm asking myself how much of that was really necessary. I tried to protect her from knowing too much about my life, which is to say that I tried to protect myself from her disappointment.

I'm a writer now. Maybe not the famous one she thought I would be, at least not yet, but regardless I'm what she thought I was. I could never tell her I didn't want to marry a woman, nor could I ever tell her that Jess wasn't actually my girlfriend. I couldn't really tell her much about my life. Definitely not that I'm a pagan, or a leftist, or about getting married to a man.

I wish I could have, which is one of the things that ancestor veneration exists to help with. I hated lying to keep up appearances, and I've lived most of my adult life such that that I never have to do that again. I also live my life such that no one feels they need to lie to me, that those I care for and those who care for me can all just be honest about who they are, and that things aren't always beautiful.

I learned to hide things about myself, and I learned that from her, but that was the wrong lesson. I've now unlearned that lesson, and I've learned that hiding yourself from others is a great way to make yourself quite miserable, and them as well.

It's a good thing my grandmother wasn't wearing her glasses when she saw that photo, and even better that Jess didn't let her keep it. In it, I'm smiling, tripping on acid, standing in front of a wall of merchandise. Several friends are in the photo, hanging out waiting for me to close the store so we can go dancing.

I don't remember why Jess took that photo, but I do remember the cover of the one video just next to my face, the details of which you could make out clearly. As I said, I worked in an adult video store—a porn shop—and next to me, in the photograph, is a picture of a woman, her eyes bright and her lips parted in a broad open smile as she is about to shove a very, very large black cock into her mouth.

The Elements of Man: A Mythic Framework for Masculinity

For any man, feminist criticisms of masculinity without corresponding guidance as to how to be better creates a sense that maybe there is something innately and unavoidably bad about being a man. In such a situation there are only two options. The first is to live, always, with a sense of Christian guilt for being a man, constantly apologizing for who you are. The second option, one many male friends of mine have chosen over the years, is to ignore all the criticisms and seek out ideological frameworks where masculinity is seen as neutral or is actually celebrated.

Unfortunately, while the second option can be extremely liberating, the frameworks available to such men are sometimes defined by the very things that feminism criticizes. While many feminist writers and websites offer very little (if any) advice on how to be "good men," there is no shortage of really bad advice on offer. Tips on how to pick up or manipulate women, the glorification of hyper-aggression or dominance over others—if you're searching for guidance on how to be a man, these things make up the bulk of your options.

Basically, what's on offer from these sources is an inverted image of feminism, a kind of immature reaction. For these thinkers, masculinity is defined by feminism—what feminists call bad or toxic, they relabel as good and sell to men looking for something deeper and more authentic.

I suspect the reason this happens is that our modern industrial civilizations did away with myth. Cultures around the world and throughout history have had their mythic models of men and masculinity. Stories and songs told of the lives of virtuous men—their actions, their struggles, their failures, and their successes. Tales were told of ancestors, heroes, leaders, warriors, tricksters, rogues, elders, mystics, as well as everyday men. Their deeds were recounted, their memories kept alive.

Even more importantly, these were not stories of one man but of many men, many kinds of men. That is, in mythic cultures there was not one story but many, many ways to be a man. Also, there were many stories of how not to be a man—myths and histories of the fate of men who caused harm, or violated sacred boundaries between human and nature, or between men and women, or between humans and the gods.

In our industrial civilization, the bard, the poet, the village elder, and the sacred story have been replaced by mass media, Hollywood films, and vapid television series that force-feed us depictions of capitalist heroes: men with new cars, or expensive technology, or well-appointed condos in exclusive urban centers. Success as a man, according to these empty myths, mostly just means success as a consumer, a soldier in service of a consumer order.

We need different myths, and we need a third road between the deadlock of feminist critique of masculinity and the "manosphere's" repackaging of those criticisms. We need this for many reasons. It does no good to paint 4 billion people as innately bad because of their sex or gender. It does feminists no good that their criticisms are increasingly ignored by men who've come to realize that feminism offers no suggestions on how to be a man, only constant reproaches for being the wrong kind of man.

I needed new myths. I struggled much of my life with being a man. For me, this was largely linked to a hatred of my body; a sense that there was nothing good about any of its masculine or male traits, and a deep despair that led to multiple suicide attempts.

Two mythic frameworks pulled me from this despair. The first was the concept of the "alchemical wedding"—the idea that it is both possible and deeply important to fully embody masculinity and femininity within the same body (regardless of sex). Just as transformative for me was the mythic framework of the elements: fire, water, earth, and air. In modern witchcraft, as well as in ancient philosophy and science, these four elements are seen as the primal forces which create and sustain the world. Everything is made up of at least one of these elements, and the more complex the thing is, the more the elements mix within and act through it.

A Crash Course on the Elements

As with the alchemical wedding, the elemental framework describes apparent opposites existing and acting together. Wind is air, of course, but it is also earth (particles of dust), water (humidity in the air), and fire (warmth). Soil is earth, but it is often also water (even dry soil has a little moisture in it, otherwise it will fly away as dust in the wind), air (the looser the soil, the more air there is), and fire (again, warmth—even frozen soil is above absolute zero).

The ocean is water but also air (fish would die otherwise), and earth (otherwise the ocean would have nothing in it), and fire (heat differences cause ocean currents). A campfire is fire, but also water (steam is released even from dry logs), earth (the wood that is burning), and air (without oxygen a fire dies).

The elements are also associated, in this framework, with certain qualities and traits in the world as well as in humans. Earth, for instance, has the qualities of stability, safety, and structure, symbolizes wealth and tradition, and is most associated with the physical body. Water has the qualities of fluidity, permeation, and dissolution, and is most associated with emotions and birth. Fire has the qualities of transformation, energy, and— as the source of light (the sun, firelight) —illumination and initiation, and is associated with the will. Air has the qualities of movement, lightness, and space, and is associated with thought and ideas in humans because of its connection to breath (to be inspired literally means to have "breathed in.")

Because the elements are seen to compose all of life and to imbue certain traits of human interactions, it's quite easy to use them to understand personality traits and stages of human development. In fact, that's why there are four suits in Tarot. Each of the suits corresponds to an element (wands are fire, cups are water, coins/pentacles are earth, and swords are air), and each of the individual cards (the aces up through the kings) represent stages or states of each element.

This same concept can apply just as easily to understanding men and masculinity, as well as women and femininity. There is no one right way to be a man or to be masculine, but rather many ways, according to what elements predominate within a man, elements which themselves are often in flux.

I here present to you an elemental framework of masculinity and men, informed by my observations and experiences of men throughout my life. No man is truly just one element, but rather a symphony of the four elements constantly mixing with and acting upon each other. However, we can often see that one or two elements tend to be at the fore, certain qualities and traits having more active roles in the formation of his personality.

These elemental frameworks act much like archetypes—unconscious roles that men take on or are influenced by at different times in their lives. A man whose masculinity is mostly formed by elemental air, for example, may find himself more shaped by elemental earth in certain reactions (with co-workers or lovers, for instance) and by elemental fire in moments of crisis.

One important thing that you'll notice is the complete absence of certain words in these descriptions, particularly the words "good" and "bad." Moral judgments don't fit within such frameworks, nor are they helpful. There is no "good" way to be a woman—nor is there a "bad" way—specifically because there is no one way to be a woman. It is the same for men.

Instead of moral judgments, I offer suggestions on how each element may clash with, feel unhelpful to or be mistaken as "toxic" by others. Problematic moral judgements arise in our modern industrial societies in which all people—men and women—are reduced to worker and consumer. In other ways of organizing societies, it was recognized that men have as many diverse needs as women, and without ways to fulfill those needs or find meaningful places in society, helpful traits can become harmful.

For example, societies that have rituals of courting create spaces for men and women to meet, flirt, and enact their passions and desires in a way that the community can celebrate and be sustained by. These societies acknowledge the traits and qualities of adolescents and provide space for them rather than suppressing such things, with the deep awareness that suppressed or repressed forces and desires always find a way to manifest. The desire for adventure, or to be a protector, or to struggle against others, are often traits found in masculinity, and societies that provide outlets, roles, and rituals in which these desires can be enacted are less likely to find bored men causing havoc or destruction.

Finally, as this is a mythic framework, it's important to say something about the mythic itself. Because we do not live in a culture that understands the importance of myth, we can sometimes forget that the mythic is neither true nor false. The mythic can only be fully understood by the same part of our mind that understands poetry.

In poetry, there is never a one-to-one correspondence between a word and its meaning. Instead, each word builds upon the words previous and the words that come after, and the poet chooses words not only for their sound but also for their multiple meanings. Like herbs added to a soup, or subtones and overtones in musical composition, each word adds not just a primary sense but a secondary sense which, when combined with other secondary senses, creates another realm of meaning inaccessible otherwise.

Put another way, the mythic is the exact opposite of math, in which each number signifies one thing and one thing only. In reading this elemental framework, do not approach it like math, but rather like poetry. It is neither untrue nor true, but both, and also something else entirely.

The Man of Elemental Earth

You know the kind of guy who never seems to dwell on his emotions, or think too deeply about a matter? Who seems maddeningly calm when others are upset, who shrugs his shoulders at things others in his life think are world-ending crises? Who, when something goes wrong goes for a run, or spends hours in the garage or the backyard doing work instead of talking things through with his partner, his family, or his friends?

This is a man of elemental earth.

Earth is structure, stability, practicality, and pragmatism. Earth traits can seem boring to others, or un-intellectual, or conservative, leading others to think a man of elemental earth is stupid, stubborn, slow-witted, or emotionally immature. But a man of elemental earth has learned something about existence that the rest of us tend to forget. We are physical bodies, with physical needs, and those bodies are very good at managing most of the crises that arise from life.

The man of elemental earth knows a nap or a jog or a good meal can be just as effective—if not even more so—as talking through problems when responding to life's inevitable turns and troubles. When you have a roof over your head, a full stomach, and some savings in the bank, life is a lot easier.

The man of elemental earth seems to have an intuitive sense of the body that the rest of us only learn through meditation, therapy, or other forms of self-help. All emotions—anxiety, fear, depression, happiness, desire—arise from the body and exist there. Difficult emotions are "all in your head," and the best way to deal with them is to get out of your head and into the rest of your body. Doing something with his hands, or his feet, going to the gym, or hiking, or having sex, or just experiencing something physical is the way this man does that.

Earth is and symbolizes the material, which includes the materialistic. The man of elemental earth is a worker, whether for others or for himself. "An honest day's work" is not just a saying for the man of elemental earth, but a kind of spiritual truth. Work feels good and true to him, especially work that puts his body to full use. He is a construction worker, a farmer, a gardener, a logger, a sanitation worker, and all those other "salt of the earth" jobs that keep the world running. Such men and the jobs they work are often seen as low-class, crude, and stupid, but civilization would collapse without them.

The man of elemental earth is conservative, though not necessarily politically conservative. He'd rather figure out how to survive in this world than risk his life and abandon those that depend on him for the utopian fantasies of others. He doesn't necessarily like the way things are, but he doesn't see the point in wishing things were different when he's got a family to feed and limited time on earth to experience life.

That conservatism translates into saving, into cautious investments in tangible things (reliable cars, well-built homes) and people (direct family members, close friends) rather than abstract causes, get-rich schemes, foreign ventures, or high-risk stocks. If he opens a business, it will be one that has a traditional and societally-useful role—a store selling basic goods, a restaurant offering reliable and uncomplicated fare, a mechanic's garage—rather than a venture marketed as the "next big thing."

A man of elemental earth is the most reliable person in your life, providing what you rely on him for his practical advice, a strong hug, help with a construction project, or the loan of his truck. It's important to realize, though, that this reliability comes from the same place that makes him seem boring, stupid, thoughtless, or unemotional to others. He likes being useful and needed, he prefers and needs clear goals and directions, and he judges others not according to their morals or status but by their actions and stability.

He doesn't like head games, emotional drama, or unnecessary tears, because none of that gets anything done. He can seem "toxic" or heartless to others—especially women—who might not have the same experience of elemental earth. Telling him, "You should have known what I wanted," or "I shouldn't need to ask you," is useless, because he doesn't operate in the realm of subtle cues and nuance.

He can seem stubborn and even stern or harsh to his children, especially if the society they live in has changed radically between the time of his youth and theirs. His life probably looks a lot like his parents' life did, because he saw what worked for them and adopted those things as his own. But if his children want something completely different or are swept up by new ideas he doesn't understand or trust, they might become hostile to him, rebelling against his legacy for years until, decades later, they may find themselves wishing they'd understood him better. Even still, the man of elemental earth will bail his alienated and hostile children out of jail or help them pay medical bills—though he won't lend them money to buy things he knows they don't really need.

Because of his loyalty, his conservative nature, his stability, and his calm demeanor, he makes a good protector, defender, and soldier. This last role is where the man of elemental earth is the most likely to be exploited by more powerful men of other elements. If he joins the military, he does so out of a sense of duty, a desire to be useful, and a need to make sure those he cares for are safe. He doesn't join for ideological reasons, because he doesn't live by ideas, and that will often keep him in the lowest ranks of any hierarchy. Thus, he's more likely to be the first to be sent out to die as cannon fodder by generals and politicians.

There is a kind of quiet enjoyment of simple things in the life of a man of elemental earth. He's the guy who plays darts with his buddies at the bar or throws around a football with his friends or kids, or goes on long camping trips with his partner. He also tends to enjoy being around family a lot more than other men do, and he isn't very likely to talk politics with them or really with anyone. He understands friendships and relationships to be built around presence, being a body amongst other bodies, sharing meals or long summer afternoons at the beach or in the backyard with others.

If he uses crass language or makes crude jokes, it isn't because he is trying to shock anyone. Instead, he's just speaking the language of those around him, adapting to the social framework in which they all exist. Out of those contexts, however, this adaptation can be seen as offensive, sexist, or racist, or accrue various other moral judgments, especially if he has moved from a rural setting, with closer community ties, to the alienating urban.

That's why men of elemental earth are so misunderstood by people who judge others according to their speech or ideas. Such ideological frameworks are often incomprehensible to those who don't prioritize the mental at the expense of the physical. On the other hand, men of elemental earth are the most reliable union members you'll ever find, because they value hard work and fair compensation much more than they value esoteric theories and academic frameworks.

The Man of Elemental Air

My really awesome 10-year-old nephew is a "mansplainer."

"Mansplaining," is a term coined by Rebecca Solnit to define a problem she felt she encountered everywhere. In her book, *Men Explain Things To Me*, she bemoans the experience of men telling her things she already knows as if she were an uneducated idiot and they felt some duty to enlighten her. As I said, my 10-year-old nephew is just such a mansplainer. He'll explain anything to you, tell you how everything works. He has a story for and a fact about everything (often but not always true) and he has composed a long instructional video in his head answering any question you might have for him and many that you don't.

It's not that he and the many other men like him are trying to be rude. It's just that they're all men of elemental air.

Air symbolizes mind, thought, spaciousness, the intellect, and movement. It's communication, and the invisible vibrations called sound and radio waves that bring words and information to our ears over vast distances. Air is a library, the internet, a university, the Greek *agora*—open spaces full of ideas, histories, theories, and all the trivia humans have ever collected and shared with each other.

The man of elemental air loves ideas and mental objects, not because they are useful but because they are interesting. Unlike the man of elemental earth, practicality and pragmatism are the farthest things from his mind. Fantasy football statistics, the dates and casualties of skirmishes during the Napoleonic Wars, agricultural output changes after the introduction of nitrogen fertilizer to India, the calorie and protein content of each one of the 1500 or so French cheeses, the incarceration rate of Black or Indigenous youth in the United States since 1956, or the top five yearly contenders in the Eurovision Song Contest since its founding: It doesn't matter if these facts are useful or not, he'll know them if they're interesting to him.

He doesn't collect data and memorize dates and statistics to show that he is intelligent or to prove something to anyone. He just does it because it's what he does. Anything he turns his mind to is absorbed quickly. And because air is not just thought but also movement, the man of elemental air is always compelled to share the wealth of knowledge he has accumulated because to him that's exactly what it is: wealth.

"Knowledge is power" is one of his founding beliefs, and he's right. Those who know more than others can react more quickly to crises, can trace the movement of historical forces, and can get better deals in economic transactions. "Ignorance is bliss," on the other hand, is pure blasphemy to the man of elemental air. And do not say "a penny for your thoughts" to such a man, because you'll get much more in return for that small investment than you'll know what to do with.

Men of elemental air make excellent professors, instructors, scientists, consultants, bureaucrats, and technocrats. The internet is their invention, as is television, and radio, and all other methods of communication. Anything that moves or spreads an idea brings them joy.

In Tarot, air is represented by the sword, which reveals another aspect of these men: They love conflict. They love to argue and to debate, not out of a desire for dominance or power, but merely for the pure joy of sharpening wit. In the process they learn which ideas are the most durable, the strongest, the most powerful, and the most interesting.

If they play sports, they tend to do so competitively. Unlike the man of elemental earth, they don't engage in the physical out of a sense of bodily joy, but rather an intellectual drive to increase, push limits, and sharpen their skills. This drive makes them just as likely to play video or board games as to become Mixed Martial Arts fighters.

The man of elemental air knows how things work, not necessarily from experience but often because he read about it somewhere and remembered. He can usually figure out how to fix whatever's broken, but he might use duct tape and forget to put a screw or two back in at the end.

Which points to something anyone who has ever loved a man of elemental air knows intimately—he cares nothing for perfection, at least in others. He's the most permissive and open-minded of all the types of elemental man, more interested in how you came to an idea than whether that idea is morally upstanding or socially acceptable. Tradition bores him. If there is a "way it's always been done," he thinks that means it's definitely high time to try a new way.

Because of his relationship to the realm of ideas, he innately grasps something about the human condition that others take a long time to understand (if they ever do): ideas, opinions, and beliefs don't define us. They're like clothes we wear and can change or take off any time we want. That makes him deeply tolerant of others, even people with ideas and beliefs that others find morally repugnant or evil. This tolerance derives from elemental air's trait of spaciousness. A man of elemental air can step back from a situation and see things from an emotional distance (an ability some—especially women—inaccurately read as heartlessness or cold rationality). This lets him separate out his current feelings and prejudices about a person or situation from the situation itself, and therefore shift his perspective.

"I can see where you're coming from" is a true statement often uttered by the man of elemental air—he can actually see this in his mind's eye. But just because he sees how others came to their conclusions or perceptions doesn't mean he agrees with them, only that he understands and values the right of everyone to think for themselves.

His friendships often reflect this impartial view of humanity. He is likely to have women friends as well as men, and friends outside of his social class as well as from within. These friends might not necessarily like or even ever know each other, because what connects them to the man of elemental air is always something specific and peculiar, only perceived as universal by him.

He's the man who's most likely not to have noticed his partner cut their hair, or is wearing a new item of clothing, or that there is some unspoken emotional state written across their face. This isn't because he doesn't care about others or is refusing to do "emotional labor," but because he doesn't dwell in the realm of such physical signifiers. He cares about the thoughts of others, their ideas, and their personalities, not their looks or social status or even their emotional states, a maddening quality to those who spend effort, money, and energy improving such superficial signifiers.

The man of elemental air is a thinker, a communicator, a learner, and a teacher. He's often employed as a journalist, a writer, a consultant, or a trainer, especially in office jobs where the labor is primarily mental. His ability to see things from different perspectives and access intellectual distance is particularly sought-after for exploitation by the powerful, because he makes a good strategist. In addition, his ability to accumulate and sift vast amounts of information proves terrifyingly useful in legal matters and in the crafting of political platforms and laws.

His ability to hold so much knowledge in his head can serve his community, friends, and family in ways that endure far beyond his own lifespan, however. He is the bringer of new ideas and inspiration, of sciences and new skills and, in many societies, he has acted as the historian and spokesman of the people, bridging the distance of time through his ability to see beyond the immediacy of the present.

His friends, family, children, and partners love him for the very same qualities that sometimes frustrate them about him. He's the guy who tells "dad jokes" and the same story you've already heard many times before. His tolerance and acceptance of multiple perspectives can sometimes seem disloyal to those who wish he would take their side in disputes, yet these very traits make those he loves feel that they will always be loved regardless of their faults. He makes very few demands on those he loves, which can feel like a lack of attention to those accustomed to more straightforward expectations. For others, however, his love feels like pure, liberating acceptance and freedom.

The Man of Elemental Water

Every Hollywood depiction of a man—whether he is a hero or a villain, a soldier or a criminal, a romantic lover or a serial killer, a raucously funny fool or a profoundly serious intellectual or inventor, a superhero, a commoner, a king, a boy wizard, or an ancient sage, has one thing in common: They were all depicted by men of elemental water.

Water is fluidity. Pour water into a glass and it becomes that shape. Boil it into steam and it expands to fill a room. Freeze it and it becomes hard as rock.

Water reflects. The first mirrors humans ever knew were still pools and puddles that showed them not just themselves but the sky and trees above them.

Water permeates, soaks through the earth and the sky. It dissolves and erodes, over aeons wearing down the most stubborn mountains and crumbling land into the sea. It absorbs and laughs at all our efforts of aggression. Bomb the oceans and all you get is a large splash. Punch a river and all you'll get is wet.

Water is associated with emotion and feelings, but to understand why, we need to know something about the word emotion itself. In English, emotion has only meant "feelings" for the last 200 years. Before then, an emotion (*ex-movere* in Latin, "moving outward") was an extreme agitation: anger that became rage, happiness that became mania, sadness that became suicidal despair. More importantly, the word "feeling" (as well as "sentiment," the other word in use before "emotion" came to mean what it does now) referred to something that was physically felt. What we call emotions were previously understood to be things outside of us, things that swept over us temporarily and were felt by our senses, rather than originating from within.

This explains why elemental water is linked to emotion. When we go for a swim, we are immersed in water but we do not dissolve. When a wave passes over us, we are soaked but then we dry off. When a torrent of rain falls the streets are soaked and may flood, but then all that water flows away and evaporates.

The man of elemental water understands this innately. While the man of elemental earth prefers to run or work until an emotions pass, the man of elemental water swims and surfs through them. Both understand that emotions are temporary states, but only the man of elemental water comprehends the shift and flow of feelings.

That's why elemental water is associated with the arts, with poetry, dance, acting, music, and all the other ways humans shape sound, light, and movement into moments of passion. An actor can be anyone he wants to be because he knows that every human being experiences the same passions, just as the same rain falls upon everyone in the world.

Water is an animating element. Take all the bones out of a human body and it'd be a plump blob but take all the water out and we'd be left with a shriveled husk. Water a wilted plant and watch it, within hours, reach again for the sky. Irrigate a dried field and see it spring to life, weeks later, with blossoms. The man of elemental water animates. He gives life to parties, to friendships, to his family. He laughs and the sorrow of others flees from them. He cries and those around him feel his sadness too.

The man of elemental water is the classic romantic. He says just the right thing and he has won your heart. He makes just the right, subtle gesture and even the most frigid can find themselves suddenly tearing his clothes off with your teeth.

If you want a man to understand your emotions and feel with you, then you want a man of elemental water. But there is a catch: He has emotions too. While the man of elemental air possesses an innate sense of equality in the realm of ideas, the man of elemental water possesses the equalizing trait of water. The tide that rushes out will always rush in again, and water always seeks an equilibrium of exchange.

Here is where many of the feminist criticisms of masculine emotions miss something profound: There is no one "right" way to experience an emotion. While the men of elemental air and elemental earth may seem emotionally stifled or repressed, the man of elemental water is often criticized for centering his own emotions. Whether expressing sadness or rage or delight, these men are often labeled egotistical, unstable, or self-centered by those who do not understand the way they experience emotions.

The problem here is that in modern industrial society, masculine emotions are accepted only when they are useful. This is as true in the conservative "patriarchal" parts of society as it is in the feminist and progressive parts. The passionate man is seen as dangerous unless his passions can be channeled, be that in the service of nationalism, consumerism, religion, or social justice. Outside of some perceived utility, passion in men is seen as a fearful, dangerous thing that must be controlled, redirected, or destroyed.

This is particularly harmful for such men when applied to their sexuality—whether same sex, opposite sex, or any-sex attraction. Ancient cultures, especially the less patriarchal ones, had rituals and traditions around courtship. Games, dances, ruses, masquerades, and other forms of dramatic and passionate rites existed (and still exist in many cultures) in which men played out the mythic and archetypal role of the seducer. Such dramas created channels for masculine emotions and sexual desire within frameworks defined by the communities of which they were a part.

Holdouts of such rituals still exist, even in European cities. I've been witness to two such community rituals, both in Germany. The first involved a tradition where a single man was "forced" to sweep the steps of the village church on his 30th birthday. All the single women of the village who were looking for eligible men would then "co-incidentally" gather in the square in front of the church, watching his performance, and commenting on his body and buttocks as he worked. Another such ritual, also in Germany, requires that an unmarried man stand on the street corner and hang a pair of just-purchased woman's underwear from a post. Women who pass and take interest in the man can then claim the underwear as their own, but only if they can fit it over their clothes. What follows then is a scripted discussion about how the underwear actually belongs to his future wife, a script the women already know because it's the very point of the ritual.

These rituals create moments in which a man seeking a partner can act out his desire and passion in front of the community in ways that women are invited (but never forced) to participate in. Our industrial societies have no such community rituals. The passions of men have no outlet except the drunken, raucous Friday night clubs in urban centers, filled also with single women who have few other opportunities to meet single men. Without the ritualistic elements of community courtship, however, the chaos of such meetings can be disorienting, unsatisfying, and sometimes abusive.

The man of elemental water, of all the types of elemental men, is most harmed by this lack of ritual. His passions cannot flourish and create the way they want to, and so his desires meet resistance and even sometimes cause harm. Other men are harmed by this situation, because it is the man of elemental water who helps them feel more comfortable with their own passions. And women of course are also harmed, because the frameworks which empowered them to stand as equals in passion are long forgotten.

Most of all, the man of elemental water is a man of family and community. He is the animating force that brings life to others, he supports partners and children through their emotions, their sorrows, and their joys. He makes us laugh, and cry, and moan, and sigh at all the things that can be felt in the world. His innate ability to care and feel makes him a great therapist or nurse, just as his ability to embody emotion makes him a great artist and actor. In industrial society, however, such roles are only valued when they support capitalism and consumption, compensated only when the feelings a man of elemental water can convey to us inspire us to buy more.

The Man of Elemental Fire

Fire is change. Fire is transformation. Fire is initiation.

There is a moment, every year at the end of a long winter, after months of sluggish life, fatigue, and chill. Suddenly, as if in a dream, a beam of sunlight hits the skin in a way we had forgotten it could, and everything changes. We come to life again, awaken into a new understanding and a thirst for life that we had set aside as the previous year faded.

This is the power of the man of elemental fire. He does not just bear the spark of life, but he is that spark, an electric presence, a living fire that can warm even the coldest of souls.

While the man of elemental water is an artist or an actor, the man of elemental fire is a performer and a rockstar—even if he makes no art at all. His life itself is a kind of art, a living poetry, a distant call from another world, ancient or not yet born. Though he is a rockstar and a performer, he is rarely the center of attention. You've been to one of his parties, full of people having the time of their life without even knowing who their host is. You've been to the events he puts on—the concerts he promotes or the cultural spaces he creates—but you probably weren't aware they were so carefully created.

This is the grace and power of elemental fire. In Tarot, fire is represented by the wands. The figure of the knight of wands is a perfect metaphor for what such a man is. He is the revolutionary and the rebel, the man who rushes in and then just as quickly disappears, off to champion a new cause, leaving a changed landscape in his wake.

While the man of elemental water is often employed in artistic or caregiver positions, you're most likely to encounter a man of elemental fire behind a bar pouring you drinks or pulling espresso. He's taking your order in the restaurant and you can't tell if he's flirting or just doing his job. Regardless, he just made you feel beautiful and very, very alive.

He's also the guy they put up on stage to entertain you between acts, or the man stuck with the job of telling everyone that their boss is laying them off, the president is declaring war, or your mother just died in the hospital. While the man of elemental air is good at communicating information, the man of elemental fire is good at convincing you that information is true.

Fire is often associated with will and with spirit—the force within humans that manifests our ideas and desires in the world around us. That's why you'll find many men of elemental fire tend to possess a kind of unshakeable faith, whether that is faith in religious truths, gods, science, humans, or just faith in themselves.

They are as likely to be deeply religious as they are to be deeply anti-religion, and in either case they take on the role of the "firebrand" or true believer, seeking to reveal a better way of being. The atheist who believes that religion is the cause of too much suffering in the world burns with elemental fire, as does the devout New Ager who believes meditation can raise the consciousness of humanity to a new level of existence. But because elemental fire is also change, it's rare to find such a man holding to the same beliefs his entire life (a trait more often found in men of elemental earth).

This intensity, coupled with a tendency toward constant change, can seem like hypocrisy, instability, and shallowness to those who do not understand such men. But it isn't really all that hard to understand if you have ever watched a fire for more than a few minutes. Its shape is never the same, but it is always the same fire.

The friends, family, and community of a man of elemental fire not only learn to understand his nature but thrive because of it. He reminds them what is possible when they lose hope, "lights a fire under the ass" of his children when they fall into patterns of passive inaction and has little patience for people who prefer to wallow in despair. This can make him seem harsh or uncaring, especially to people accustomed to blaming other people, or structural oppression, for their poor material conditions.

Of the four elemental men, he's the one you're most likely to see out in the streets during protests, but not for the entire event. As soon as he realizes the revolution isn't going to happen this afternoon, he's off doing something else.

Because of his charisma he is often in leadership positions, even though this isn't always the best role for him. The man of elemental fire does best when an action has immediate and significant results. He's not a long-term planner (that's the province of air and earth), and can sometimes get pushed from below, from above, or by his own impatience to make decisions that have unintended consequences.

This can be a problem, especially when hierarchies are obscured by ideology. "Leaderless" movements always have leaders, and those leaders are often men of elemental fire. But without community support and clear expectations, they can find themselves chained to the weight of other people's faith, either breaking under the pressure or wielding that power in unhelpful ways.

This often leads to the feminist criticisms of "activist men" who don't seem to take responsibility for their actions or listen to "the community." What is missed here is that such men—often men of elemental fire—rarely intend to set themselves up as leaders or even notice that anyone else sees them that way. They are men of action, and their actions draw our attention. Soon they have a following, people looking to them for guidance on what to do or how to change the world, even though they never asked the rest of us to set them up on pedestals.

This explains so much of the disappointment people express when their "heroes" don't live up to their expectations. In our modern industrial societies, bereft of community rituals or mythic frameworks, we mistake our admiration for people, and the hope they inspire in us, with an unfounded sense of mutual obligation and connection.

While the man of elemental fire often becomes an activist, he's just as likely to become a gang leader. He's also just as likely to be a politician decrying the violence and destruction that gangs and political protests cause. Any role in which his will and influence are valued, and seen as useful traits, can appeal to him, depending on what belief system he currently embraces. This also makes him the man most likely to feel stifled by the docility, traditionalism, and lack of opportunity provided for men such as himself in capitalist societies, especially if he has no resources. "Male criminality" is the inevitable result of societies that devalue and actively attempt to suppress masculine fire desires for adventure and intensity.

On the other hand, most extreme sports seemed designed specifically with such men in mind. If there is any danger or risk involved, he's going to be interested. As a child, he was the kid always falling from trees, skinning his knee, breaking his arms, and getting stung by insects. This can be maddening for his mother or for partners later on, but he learned something early in life that the rest of us often did not: No risk, no fun.

He learns this through experience and learns to conquer his fears by constantly failing. Children who fall from heights very often do something completely counter-intuitive: they lose their fear of falling. This is because their bodies learn to rely on other senses than sight to gauge distance, while adults who were cautious children—obeying their parent's warning not to climb too high—become afraid and disoriented at great heights.

By rebelling and by failing, the man of elemental fire learns what he and others are truly capable of. That spark of wisdom he holds is what lights the lives of others on fire, initiating them into new realities and ways of being.

Returning to Yourself

I've come to a place where I find myself rejecting ideological overlays in favor of more pragmatic and embodied understandings of the world. It wasn't an easy place to come to, but I've had a leg-up in this understanding. I've been working with a Tantric therapist for the last year and a half. I started working with him a month after I (literally) fled an abusive relationship and realized that, while that person is fully responsible for his behavior and abuse, I abandoned a significant amount of my own, albeit unacknowledged, agency as well.

As I described to my therapist at our first meeting, that abusive relationship was a perfect storm of all of my shitty beliefs about myself and all the ideological overlays that led me repeatedly into such situations. While that relationship was by far the most abusive, I had previously been in several relationships that were not good for me. Close friends remarked on this pattern, noting that I seemed to "lose" myself quickly, when I fell in love, and soon found it incredibly difficult to get myself back again.

This way of looking at abusive relationships is not a popular framework. The grand narratives around abuse speak to larger systems (patriarchy, misogyny, etc.) at the expense of specifics. This is particularly damaging for men in abusive relationships, for whom these narratives do not account, since men are supposed to be the abusers, never the victims.

Anyone looking at the agency and patterns of the person suffering the abuse meets with wailing accusations of "victim blaming," despite the goal of such attention being to help the victimized person regain the agency they lost because of the abuse.

As I worked with this therapist, a flood of shitty self-beliefs quickly came to the surface, leading to a really rough few months for me. Much like the pain of resetting a broken bone—or physical therapy to correct movement problems caused by injuries—everything that came up felt like a new trauma. It was the pain of finally confronting myself and the beliefs I'd adopted. Those beliefs had numbed the important pain that tells you something is wrong, opiating the soul when a sober accounting was needed instead.

Once you start rejecting those old narratives, life gets difficult for a bit. The crutches you relied on won't help you climb mountains, and you've suddenly realized that you want to climb them. All the things that you told yourself you didn't like or want or desire suddenly show up with a vengeance, staring you in the face, taunting you to embrace them like the true lovers they always were. You abandoned them, and yourself, turned away from all that you really wanted, because it was easier to wallow in self-pity and complain to others about your life, or relationships, or material conditions.

When you start this process, life gets difficult but then it gets brilliant, because you start making changes in how you relate to yourself and how you relate to others. You start setting boundaries to protect your time and energy and body, and you start enforcing those boundaries. You start demanding more from others: The same respect and effort you give them, you demand in return. When they don't reciprocate that respect and effort, you stop giving it to them.

You stop being a martyr and you stop being a savior. When others demand that you take responsibility for their lives, you decline. When others demand authority over your life, you refuse them.

You step back into your agency, which is a double-edged sword you learn not to fear. When others claim that your life and actions are oppressing or harming them, you ask for concrete examples. When you feel the life and actions of others are oppressing or harming you, you force yourself to look for concrete examples as well. Often there are none, just a sense of harm and oppression you or they have been using to cover feelings of insufficiency.

You stop blaming others for your failures and self-defeating patterns, which means you stop letting others blame you for theirs. You begin to see how so many others have turned *ressentiment* into a religion, and you begin to see all the shrines to *ressentiment* you've raised in your own soul.

You become yourself again.

And this does something wild and unexpected—but utterly inevitable—for those around you: They become themselves, too. Suddenly, the people you love and who love you dance to the same unheard music you are dancing to. Instead of constantly tripping each other up, you begin teaching each other to dance, to live, to be.

Of course, you have to leave some people. You have to let them go, just as those with good boundaries had to leave you, too, until you figured it out. Some will come back to themselves, just as you finally came back to yourself. Others never will, and you learn there's nothing to be done about it.

Everything changes when you come back to yourself. That isn't to say that everything is perfect, or even better, initially, but you understand now how to change things for yourself. You also understand how impossible it is to change things for others unless they come back to themselves as well.

This gives you a new perspective on all the grand political narratives about how the world works. You start to see their core truths, and how those truths got buried under so much dogma and *ressentiment*. The core truth of Marxism, for example, is that the material conditions of humans determine the rest of their lives, with the goal of returning agency to those actually creating the wealth in society. The core truth of anarchism is that individuals can make better decisions about their lives than a state can, with the goal of returning agency to the individual. The core truth of feminism is that women are active and equally powerful co-creators of the world, with the goal of returning agency to women. The core truth of critical race theory is that the historical oppression of black people has suppressed their sense of self and humanity, with the goal of returning agency to black people.

In all these cases, the goal was to return agency. But Marxism became an excuse for many to displace their own agency onto The Party or the "vanguard." Anarchism became an excuse to displace responsibility for personal failure onto invisible structures. Feminism and critical race theory became excuses to blame men and white people for all the problems in the world.

I suspect the core truths of these grand narratives can be salvaged. I even think they can all be redeemed. This can only happen, however, if the people who have embraced them learn to embrace their own agency and return to themselves. That is the only way to strip these ideological overlays of the opiate of *ressentiment* and recenter them in what is actually capable of change, what is actually worth fighting for.

It's possible, however, that these core truths cannot be salvaged. *Ressentiment* is one hell of a drug. Like other opiates, it makes you feel good in your misery—numbs all that pain—but also makes you an awful person. A friend of mine, an ex-heroin addict, often recounted the time one of his friends died from an overdose. He spent an hour searching through the dead woman's pockets for her stash, getting angrier and angrier as he realized that she'd "selfishly" injected it all into her veins. The moment he realized that he was shaking down a corpse rather than mourning a friend's death was the moment that he finally tried to stop.

What will it take for others to awaken from *ressentiment*, this drug that tells you that you are special because you suffer, you are sacred because you are oppressed, you are worthy because you are a victim? What does it take for the fascist, for the white nationalist, for the anti-semite, for the rabid anti-immigrant to kick the habit of *ressentiment*? Because it's the same drug, the same process. Defining yourself in reference to what you hate and who you believe hates you—casting yourself into a cosmic fantasy in which hordes of unbelievers or barbarians are threatening your enclave of enlightenment—is no more truthful and no less ridiculous whether you think the enemy is cis-hetero-white-patriarchy or Islamification.

What it will take is something both simple and terrifyingly difficult: returning to yourself. Returning to your body, to your agency, to your ability to shape and change and inhabit your own life. Because once you are yourself again, you'll see others as themselves. Not as identities, not as oppressor categories, not as faceless enemies "selfishly" keeping something from you.

You will only know what is holding you back when you've learned what you are capable of. You'll find that, mostly, what has been holding you back is you; your fear, your anxiety, your lack of will, your refusal to try. Once you learn this, you will see the actual fences and barriers that exist outside of yourself, the natural and man-made limits beyond which you are not permitted to travel.

There actually are systems and collusions put in place to prevent you, to stop you, to hold you back, to ensure that immense power and wealth only rest with a few. These systems rely on the very thing that has turned all of our once-liberating ideologies into circuses of fear. These systems rely on you never knowing what you are capable of, never seeing your own agency, and never embracing the divine and creative and destructive beauty of who you really are.

Settling

> Do you have the patience to wait
> till your mud settles and the water is clear?
> Can you remain unmoving
> until the right action arises by itself?
> *Tao Te Ching*, 15

I've always been fascinating by something that happens after a period of sickness or extreme pain: You're sick, and everything's excruciating. You cannot breathe, or you have no energy. A fever is ravaging your body, your throat is sore, your stomach revolts against anything you offer it. You cannot sleep, or you cannot do anything but sleep.

You think it will never end.

Something awful is happening to you, or to those around you. Everything is panic, crisis. Fear and anxiety are coursing through you, bleeding into your every expression. Those you care for, and those who care for you, cannot bear what is happening, their shoulders breaking just like yours.

It's all too much, and you cannot imagine a moment when it won't be.

And then it's over, and the worst thing imaginable is suddenly an inaccessible memory, a ghost of a recollection. We can conjure a memory of being in pain, but we cannot recollect the actual pain itself. We remember that the crisis was terrible, but we can't hold that terror in our hearts again, even if we wanted to.

Try to remember the worst pain you've ever experienced, and try to inhabit that feeling again. Try to feel what you felt, how really horrifying it was.

You cannot.

You can get close, of course. Much like, when delving into your lushest memories of sexual encounters, you might feel aroused but you cannot replicate exactly what that feeling was like. Remember the best meal of your life, or the most glorious day at the beach or in the forest—you can only feel what it was like to have had that experience, you cannot feel the experience itself.

There are technical and psychological terms for this process, and also a few esoteric ones, but my favorite word for it is "settling."

"Settling" is a word that comes from two completely different roots that later intertwined. One example of this phenomenon is the English word "property," which derives from two different Latin words that came to be pronounced the same way in Middle French and thus merged.

"Settling" is another such merger. It derives from Anglo Saxon ("Old English") *setl* and from old Norse *satt* (which later became *sahtlen*). The two words have different but complementary meanings. *Setl* was "a seat," which the extra meaning of "home" or "abode," and was used to describe a place that a person might sit but also the position a star, the moon, or a planet in the night sky. *Satt* was also a noun, but it meant "reconciliation," as in after an argument or war.

Both meanings carry over into our modern English usage of the word "settle." It continues to refer to the act of sitting or being at rest, as in when we speak of settlers and settlements, or when we say "my stomach has settled" or "the cat settled down for an afternoon nap." The second meaning, from the old Norse, resurfaces when we speak of a court settlement or say "we need to settle this."

The latter meaning led to a negative connotation that arose in English during World War II. The word began to be used to describe the act of accepting less than you want—as in "settling for a lower wage"—the opposite of the original meaning, which held various connotations of contentment.

Regardless, I think "settling" is the best word for the process I described earlier. One reason lies in the word's inverse, "unsettling." Something is unsettling when it disturbs you, puts you out of a sense of ease, pulls you from a state of rest, or literally forces you from your seat. "Unsettling" maintains one of the otherwise lost meanings of the Old English word *setl*, that of celestial bodies having a true "seat" somewhere in the sky. Earthquakes are unsettling specifically because the earth itself is unsettled. Major disasters (from Latin, "ill star") are unsettling because the world and the heavens themselves seem to be shaken up. Unsettling things disturb us (also Latin, meaning "disorder" or "agitate").

All this points to a rather beautiful aspect of ancient Pagan cosmology that mirrors a core truth in Taoism. Before Christianity arrived, and even centuries into Christianity's transformation of society around universalist creeds, Europe's pagans believed that each celestial body had its own purpose, simply by virtue of being where it was. That is, each star in the sky has a seat there, where it is "at home" and most able to be itself.

What's always fascinated me about this kind of cosmology is that there is no need to posit a seating arrangement. That is, no one put the stars there or made places for them, because no one needed to tell the stars where they should be or what they should do. The stars just exist, they are, in an unquestioned and unquestionable act of being.

In this Pagan cosmology, the goal of human life isn't to unseat or dethrone the stars or the gods, but rather to find our own seats and our own homes. Everything in nature is in its *setl*: the forest is where the forest is, the river is flowing through its home, the stars and the sun are following their own tracks across the sky just as the deer follow their own tracks across the land.

Everything is following its own kind of order, an order arising from being rather than purpose. Purpose implies design, an ultimate destiny, what you were "put on this earth for." Being, on the other hand, is its own fulfillment, which is also the *Tao* of the *Tao Te Ching*.

Taoism is ultimately about finding the *setl*, the seat of yourself, your resting place from which true action can arise. When I first read the *Tao Te Ching*, I was a young revolutionary anarchist, full of rage, fury, and desire to remake the world. I remember being really fucking angry when I read it, finding it obnoxiously smug and condescending:

> Do you want to improve the world?
> I don't think it can be done.
> The world is sacred
> It can't be improved.
> If you tamper with it, you'll ruin it.
> If you treat it like an object, you'll lose it.
> *Tao Te Ching*, 29

Everything around me felt wrong. Everything needed to be fixed, changed, revolutionized. My life was a revolt against everything; the people in power, the injustice everywhere, the complete unrightness of life and society. I needed to act, and I believed everyone else did too, otherwise we were all going to die.

I can smile at all this now, and I'm sure my younger self would find that smile as odious as he did the words of that tiny book of Asian philosophy. I smile now because I've learned that nothing I could possibly have done back then would have accomplished what I thought was needed, and everything I did showed me what was not possible, rather than what was.

This idea of Being—just like the philosophy of the *Tao*—can be seen to argue for complete inaction, for never doing anything. That's how I first understood it when I saw it manifested in people I admired and even envied, older people whose serenity and calm felt like utter indifference to the world. I also saw it in people my own age and younger, including a close friend who would listen to my political rants, smiling, and then suddenly give me a hug. It enraged me that he didn't seem to care about the horrors of the world, yet now I see that he was more in line with Being and the *Tao* then I understood. I was unsettled, and his sudden embraces settled me.

When I think about most political strife and rage—all the "sound and fury" of identity politics—I wish someone would intervene and give those people a hug. Not because their outraged reactions to oppression are wrong, but because they are unsettled, like I was. You cannot know how to act when you are unsettled, when you are out of yourself, when you are no longer being.

You cannot make mud settle or water become clear, you can only wait for them to do so.

Which doesn't mean no action should ever be taken. The point is that "the right action arises by itself," and that such action can only arise from a state of being, from the setl—the seat of yourself.

This is why I think "settling" is the best way to describe those moments after pain and crisis when you can no longer remember how it hurt, only that it did. Everything was unsettled, and then it settled again, which is to say that we were unsettled, and then we re-settled. Trying to act through illness is a losing battle, like trying to fight a storm of strife or chaos in our lives or in the lives of those around us. By doing so we often make it worse, like when we try to keep up our daily activities despite having a flu: We only prolong the illness that way.

I've learned that it is also possible to settle into unsettling times. I'm very rarely ill, a good fortune that seems to increase the more I settle into being body. On those rare moments when I do become sick, I actually get a bit excited, because it means I'm about to learn a new way to settle into myself.

I think gym work, in particular, has taught me this, especially the split-body training program I now use. The lower back and legs are so far removed from the Western center of the body (the brain) that learning to access their immense power feels like receiving a massive inheritance from a relative you never knew existed. The hips are literally the setl of the body: You use them to settle into a seat, and also to unsettle into standing.

The pain that comes along with strengthening these muscles is unsettling, yet that pain teaches you how to settle into it, just like illness and crisis always point you back to yourself and to the body. If you've ever done heavy leg presses and rack squats, you'll also know how this kind of work teaches you the beauty and wisdom of inaction (just try walking up a flight of stairs afterward...) and the power of "correct" action.

There's a natural way to bend that follows the body's path, just like stars follow their own paths across the night sky and deer follow their own tracks through a forest. Follow that path and you become stronger, you become more yourself. Follow a path that is not natural to the body and you're likely to be injured.

Subtle and light actions affect deep change because they arise out of rather than disturb being. The sun's warmth and light emanate from and flow through the very act of being the sun, just as our warmth and light arise from the act of being ourselves. This may sound like hippy crap or white-light drivel, yet the longer I live the more I see that there is no other beautiful way of being but this.

And this way of being requires settling. Not "settling for," but settling into. Not mere contentment or false compromise, but rather great patience, and a certainty that disturbed waters eventually become clear, storms inevitably pass, and great strife finally burns itself out. In that moment of settling—and only at that moment—we can see right action arising out of the true act of being.

The Contagion of Delight

This past weekend, on the first night of the full moon, my husband and I went to a nightclub—which is not something either of us is known for doing, at least not since we were in our 20s—and it was definitely not the sort of place we normally find ourselves in.

We needed to. I don't know how to explain except to say that it was an imperative: A response to a loud (albeit unspoken) demand that we go to a place where people are. We needed to purge from our souls the isolation, fear, and social alienation imposed upon us over the last two years.

A month ago, on my way to visit my sister, I got myself a bit lost. Normally I ride my bike to a nearby village, hop a train coming from Germany that's headed into the city, and take a tram and then a bus to wherever I'm ultimately headed. Often that's one of the small Chinese or Turkish shops where I buy all the things I cannot find in the stores near me, or to purchase clothing, but usually I'm going to visit my sister.

I know the way, yet that day everything had changed. Not the buildings, not the streets, not the transit stops, but the people, each of them suddenly wearing faces rather than masks. Just a week before, on the weekend of our wedding, the government of Luxembourg finally dropped all the masking requirements, and suddenly the streets were full of humans.

I've never been one to indulge in misanthropy. I've had friends who just really don't like people, or who are are true introverts. I'm neither, but because I am a writer I find that I'm either alone or with just one other person most of the time. And though I get easily overwhelmed when there are a lot of people around, it's because I like people so damn much and so I'm no good at closing myself off from what they're doing and saying all around me.

The last two years made me think that perhaps I wasn't really a "people person," but that's just the sort of story you tell yourself to get through. Best to tell yourself such things when there are no other options, I guess, but deep down you know it's not true and that you're really deeply disappointed and sad about it all.

The unmasking made me remember that people are fascinating and confusing and beautiful and bizarre and relentlessly interesting, even when they're completely dull. Strangers are everywhere—walking about, going on with their lives—and you get the briefest glimpse at their existence on this earth as they pass you on the street. Without masks, they all had faces again, which meant their realness was harder to ignore. More so, my own realness suddenly felt undeniable because they all saw my face, too.

A woman looked overlong at me as she approached and then passed me on the sidewalk. She smiled an interested, flirtatious smile. Even though I'm not interested in women, I couldn't stop smiling afterwards. Because I was still smiling about that encounter as I passed by and looked at other people, some of them smiled back too, spreading a contagion of delight through the day.

That's how I became lost. I knew the way, of course, but the joy and life of the crowds thronging the streets without fear of each other swept me up along other paths, and it was the best kind of being lost a human can experience.

Going to the nightclub felt the same. Good gods, the music was horrible, the whole place smelled of too many high-end French perfumes clashing together, and the dancing was embarrassingly ridiculous. That made it all the more delightful, though, because that's precisely the sort of frivolous absurdity that dissolves all the frigid and staid qualities of civilization that masking enforced. People said reckless things to each other, and dressed oddly, and most of all looked at each other the way you do—the way you have to—when you all have faces.

It's hard to forget that such gatherings were vilified during the last few years. News stories and social media posts showing images of people doing delightful things became a kind of public shaming, like how ration-cheaters were held up for public hatred during the world wars. How dare these people go on living when the rest of us can not? Crowding the beaches during a pandemic, using more than their allotment of butter: They were the reason the rest of us suffered. They were the reason the war/virus hadn't ended yet.

What I found myself thinking, at that club, was how in such places and at such moments the machine logic of political morality cannot find purchase. After all, identity itself is a mask—a way to hide the real of you from the real of others—and delight dissolves identity in the universal solvent of joy, in the relentless real.

The scourge of identititarian politics is born from the internet and the university, arenas of the abstract. That scourge escapes those laboratories, of course, stretching its miasmic tendrils into the minds of everyone infected by their discourse, but it takes a long time to truly reproduce in its victims. It might choke out the breath of other ideas for a while, but real, raw life persists beyond such suffocation.

A few days later, my husband and I hosted a very large meal at our house. It's traditional here to have a lunch the Monday after Easter, even for non-religious sorts, and this year my husband decided to invite people from our village as a way of celebrating our wedding, thanking them for their gifts, and ritualizing my arrival as part of the village. While I've lived here now for over two years, marrying a villager means I've married into the village, a completely anti-modern idea which I've come to adore.

He gets hardcore with such events. One of his favorite films (and a relentless inspiration) is *Le Festin de Babette* (Babette's Feast), a beautiful and subtle Danish film. The story is quite simple: A French woman arrives in a remote, rural village where the daughters of a Puritan prophet carry on their father's austere legacy and care for his followers. The woman is a refugee from the strife surrounding the Paris Commune and becomes their servant and cook in exchange for safety. One day the woman learns that she has won a lottery and decides to use all the money to prepare a singular Parisian feast for the village: One moment of utter delight.

Whenever my husband decides we'll invite large groups of people over, he becomes Babette. Weeks of planning and days (this time four of them) of cooking beforehand, all to create one moment of exquisite delight, rare elegance, and some of the best food you'll ever eat. And each time, just like in the film, everyone leaves feeling like aristocracy: kings and queens departing a feast in their honor.

Delight is one of the strongest magics humans have ever known, and maybe the only true antidote to alienation. This is what all those colonial and missionary accounts of indigenous contact got wrong, the ones in which the authors exclaim about how the people they encounter act like innocent "children." Childhood was probably the last time any of those writers were allowed to experience raw life fully, and thus they assume that delight is something only children experience. Their amazement is really longing and sorrow for the Real, which they stopped letting be real.

This is also the primary mechanism of *ressentiment*, the vampiric gaze endlessly animating identity strife. How dare others enjoy their own existence without constantly apologizing for who they are, without following unwritten rules about social castes and ideological structures that imprison us in our own minds? Others delight, but we cannot let ourselves delight, and therefore delight must be snuffed out of the world.

Delight is contagious, but *ressentiment* inoculates us against its virulence. Fortunately, delight mutates faster than any politics can adapt. It spreads through smiles and laughter, and like children do, it touches everything in sight. Disinfect every surface and erect as many barriers as you can, delight will eventually find a vector into your soul.

Soap Has Always Been With Us, and Longer Still

I.

We moderns have a bizarre tendency to think of the past as a place of tragedy, misery, darkness, and ignorance. Our ancestors were all stupid, living in filth, squalor, and poverty, toiling to eke out a living from the soil. I say "bizarre" because this framing is a kind of abnormality in cultural cosmologies.

We are one of the very few civilizations that look at the past this way, and the only one to have such a firm belief in time as linear progression. Which may sound strange. It's difficult to imagine another way of understanding time, and some of this difficulty derives from our language itself, or rather from the linguistic limits built into our language.

Consider what it might be like to speak a language that has no past tense, no way of differentiating between something that happened yesterday and something that happened a century ago. Imagine how you might tell a story about your child, how everything might seem to bleed into the present.

Many languages have no past tense. They have ways of speaking about events which have happened, but not of describing the past as something that no longer exists. Linguistically, the past functions like a place that you're not currently in, or a direction in which you are looking, rather than a time period that has passed.

While this might feel limiting, it's only because our own linguistic framework is also limited. When you are accustomed to thinking of time as something that travels past you, or as a road you are on that only goes in one direction, it's very difficult to conceive of a different way of perceiving time. Trapped in our linguistic prisons, we can only perceive time as a string of discrete moments which occur, once, and then end, rather than as an entire forest stretching out in all directions from where we stand.

But don't despair. There's a very simple way to escape this prison, using something that has always been with us, and longer still: Soap.

II.

Think of the past. Imagine it the way our modern delusions tell us to imagine it. Imagine what life was like a thousand years ago, or two thousand. Imagine what life was like without the ability to wash yourself or your clothes. Imagine how bad people must have smelled, how dirty everything was, how wretched everything looked, and how grimy your skin would have felt without that artifact of modern, daily life, soap.

And now realize that all your imaginings are completely wrong.

Soap has always been with us. Soap has been around as long as we have been around, and even longer. Soap isn't a new thing. Soap isn't a thing that humans invented. Soap is the offspring of fire, flesh, and water, born in the ashes of forest and cooking fires and funeral pyres.

The oldest record of soap is from Babylon, some 4800 years ago as we moderns tell time. A clay tablet bears the magic formula for the creation of a specific kind of soap, one used to clean wool so that the dye will take better. That tablet is the oldest record we have, which only means it was probably one of the first times someone decided that a specific recipe for soap needed to be chiseled into permanence.

Combine wood ash with fat and water, that tablet directs the reader. This is how soap is born, not "created" or "invented" but arising out of something else.

Cook a piece of meat over a wood fire, let the rain fall on those ashes afterward, and you have soap in its rawest form. Not the soap you might use in your shower, of course, which—especially if it's a "shower gel" or "liquid soap"—is probably actually a synthetic detergent.

Those wet, greasy, cook-fire ashes will lift greases and oils from other things. That's what soap is and what soap does. In other words, every time a human cooks meat over a wood fire, and water touches those ashes, there is soap. Soap, then, is "as old as" cooking, and older still.

Rain falling upon the remains of a dead animal burnt by a forest fire births soap, too.

We moderns want to know when soap was first "invented." We want to name the moment in human history before which there was no soap, and after which there was soap.

Soap is older than we are, though, which means we didn't make soap. We only learned its uses. We might speak of soap the way alchemists speak of things, without trapping them in the linguistic prison of linear time. Alchemists speak of "salts," the remains of a thing after fire and water have had their way with it. Salt is what remains of the sea once the water has gone, burned away by the heat of the sun.

A "salt" is what remains of wood once fire has burned it to ash, water has dissolved and purified that ash, and fire has dried away the water. The resulting salt is called potash or lye. Potash is actually two words together—"pot" and "ash"—because it is the substance remaining after ashes are leeched in water and then boiled in iron pots. Potash is the root of our word "potassium," coined in the 1800s to describe a substance that humans had always known. The chemists say that potash is an alkali, which is just to say the same thing twice: "Alkali" is the Arabic word *(al-qaliy)* that means "ash."

The other word for this alchemical salt—lye—is from an ancient Germanic word that meant "to wash." It has the same root as the English words "lather," "launder," and "latrine," and referred first to a kind of water itself (water mixed with wood ash for cleaning) rather than to the salt remaining once the water evaporated.

You can bathe in water filled with wood ash and come out feeling less oily, because lye reacts with oils in an alchemical process called "saponification." Soap is the transmutation of lye and oil into a substance that clings to and separates other oils and fats from each other.

That's how soap cleans, whether in its cruder form—as wet ashes and grease—or as the prettier and better-smelling soaps we generally think of. In water, the oils of soap bind to the oils you wish to remove, and more water carries it all away from the skin.

We are using oil to clean away oil. Which may explain why both the Chinese and the Romans tended to use only oil, or sometimes oil mixed with wood ashes, to clean themselves after bathing in water. In

Rome, this involved the use of a strigil, a curved piece of metal (often copper or brass) used to scrape the oil off the skin after first covering yourself in it. In China, unguents made with pig pancreas (or cured fish), fat, and wood ash were applied and then scraped off.

There is a popular falsehood that our word "soap" comes from a story about the mythic Roman Mount Sapo. The story goes that clothing rinsed in the streams flowing from that mountain always came out particularly clean, because burnt offerings were performed at its summit. Supposedly, soap from ritual slaughter flowed into the streams, and humans discovered it. There was no Mount Sapo, however, and the story is not a Roman myth but a much later creation. But our word "soap" does come from the Romans, who got it from the Germans. We know this from Pliny the Elder, who wrote that both the Celtic Gauls and the Germans used it:

> There is also soap (*sapo*), an invention of the Gauls for making their hair shiny. It is made from tallow and ashes, the best from beechwood ash and goat fat, and exists in two forms, solid and liquid; among the Germans both are used more by men than by women.

Like most Roman and Greek historians, Pliny never visited or even met most of the people he wrote about, rewriting other people's accounts instead. Both Gauls and Germans often had fair or even red hair, and thus the "shine" of their hair might just have referred to its color, although their hair may also have been clean because they were using soap to wash it. Regardless, at the same time that the citizens of an empire were using oil to clean themselves, the supposedly backwards, ignorant, and superstitious indigenous people (the Gauls and the Germans) were lathering themselves up with soap.

III.

The first record of soap is from Babylon, a specific kind of soap for a specific use. It's for cleaning wool, which cannot be dyed until the oils are removed. Later records, from Egypt for example, also describe how to make specific soaps for specific uses.

Folk traditions say that soap is much older, especially those in Africa and the Middle East.

Alata samina, or *ose dudu*, ("African black soap") is said to be thousands of years old. Crafted primarily by Yoruba women, it is a soap made of plant ash, water, and shea or other "butter" oils. In what is now Syria there is ghar soap, laurel soap, or more famously "Aleppo Soap." As with African black soap, its origin story is older than the Western mindset can conceive: Locals say it is at least 4000 years old, almost as old as the Babylonian recipe for wool-cleansing soap.

Whether or not you believe its origin story, Aleppo soap has a special history. It was the recipe for Aleppo soap that formed the basis of the first two mass-manufactured soaps in Europe: Castile soap and Marseille soap. Soap was in use throughout Europe long before Spanish artisans began making Castile soap and, later, French merchants began producing *savon de Marseille*, but it was the Arabs who first learned how to make soap in large amounts.

Aleppo soap uses laurel oil along with olive oil; Marseille and Castile soap do not use laurel. All three combine the ashes of halophytes—grasses and other plants that thrive along the seacoast—along with boiling water (seawater in traditional Marseille and Castile soap), then allow the soap to harden. It takes a month for Marseille and Castile soaps to be ready to use, while Aleppo soap is aged for at least six months—and sometimes up to three years—in order to be considered authentic.

Aleppo soap—along with its cousin, Nabulsi soap—was the original mass-produced soap, and it became quite popular during and after the crusades. Crusading soldiers, as well as merchants and priests, brought back sacksful of the soap to trade (and perhaps also as payment). Europe already had soap—the Celts and Germans had been making it before the Roman Empire arose—but the Arabic soap was superior in quality, harder, and therefore much longer lasting. Also, because it was made with plant oils rather than animal fat, it felt better on the skin: soaps made from animal fats are stronger and therefore more drying.

Spanish and French merchants eventually copied Aleppo soap on a very large scale, engaging in what may have been the first industrialized production scheme in Europe. Because of their military dominance, Spanish merchants spread Castile soap to England, undercutting folk soap-making there.

It was during this period, just before the birth of capitalism and industrialization, that a strange thing happened in Europe—people stopped cleaning themselves regularly. There are several reasons for this. First, Castile soap became associated with Catholicism, and Protestant leaders in England preached against using soap or even bathing nude at all. Our idea of "dirty," foul-smelling peasants comes from this period in England, when bathing was seen as a sign of idolatry and lewd behavior, rather than simple hygiene. The British Crown fed into this moral reversal by heavily taxing soap, raising the prices so high that even the rich didn't think it worth the price.

In France, now renowned for its Marseille soap, people also stopped bathing regularly. This wasn't due to moral panic, but rather "enlightenment" and "science." Doctors in the early days of the Age of Reason thought that bathing in hot water caused disease, which they concluded must enter the body through open pores. Soap was believed to open pores and clear the skin of its "protection" against foul airs. Thus, beginning with the aristocracy, the French stopped bathing regularly or using soap. Louis XIV was said to have only taken two or three baths in his lifetime and did not even like to be washed with a cloth. Despite the relentless perfumes filling the palace of Versailles to cover the poor hygiene of the entire court, the king's body odor was so bad that an Austrian official complained he smelled like a wild boar. Even today you'll find that many people in France bathe or shower quite rarely, as I found while living there.

This is why moderns have a belief that soap, personal hygiene, and regular bathing are new things, and that our ancestors were dirty and smelled bad. The story goes that people had to be convinced to use soap, that soap is a miraculous invention wrought by capitalism.

This falsehood is due to the commercialization of soap in the United States, beginning with Proctor & Gamble's chemical soap, Ivory, in 1879. Early advertising hints at the reality of the situation. Ivory was sold as an improvement on both home-made soaps as well as the Castile soap already widely available. Proctor & Gamble claimed that Ivory was a "purer" soap, despite their addition of extraneous chemicals like magnesium sulfate.

Most of the soaps in use now are not actually soaps at all, but detergents. Both function in similar ways, but detergents are created from industrial chemicals rather than natural ingredients. Detergents arose during the early 20th century due to shortages of oil and tallow, which were diverted for war efforts. Residues from coal and, later, from petroleum were the primary sources for these detergents, and now the list of chemicals used to create them is very, very long. Like many of the "new" inventions of our supposedly modern, enlightened age, detergents are more destructive and "dirtier" than their predecessors: The chemicals in most detergents do not break down over time, polluting water and damaging other parts of nature.

It's fair to say that, despite our belief that modern people are cleaner and more hygienic than our ancestors, our civilization is actually dirtier.

IV.

Soap is not the only way to get clean, of course. I've already mentioned the ancient practice of using oils. The Chinese also used fragrant wood chips, rubbing them against the skin to pick up dirt and oils. In many other cultures, especially those indigenous to the Americas, plants and leaves were used for the same purpose, after bathing in water.

In many places, water itself was enough to clean away any grime, dirt, and oil. Thermal and countless other springs are still used for bathing, as they were for thousands and thousands of years. In many cases, the water from these springs is alkaline and filled with minerals such as natron (sodium bicarbonate) or washing soda (sodium carbonate), both of which clean the skin and clothing quite well. And the ocean is full of one of the most basic cleaning elements of all: Salt. A swim in the sea will clean away grime as well as bacteria, and you don't even need to scrub at all.

Many plants themselves produce a kind of soap called "saponins" which has been used by countless cultures. The two best-known such plants were named for this quality: soapwort and soap nut. Horse chestnuts, ivy, clematis, buffalo berry, bracken fern, baby's breath, beet leaves, yucca, fenugreek, and even most beans are high in saponins and can be boiled down to create a liquid soap.

Another powerful cleaning liquid, perhaps surprisingly, is urine. Unless the person producing it is ill, urine is a sterile liquid that can be—and often was—used to clean wounds. More common, however, was the use of urine to clean particularly deep stains out of clothing, because it is high in ammonia (as such, it's also been used to whiten teeth). Urine is also the oldest recorded "mordant" used in fabric dying. After soaps were used to clear the oils from wool and linen, the cloth was soaked in urine and plant or mineral dyes. The urine held the dyes in the cloth.

It may not be necessary to clean yourself regularly, depending on what you eat. Body odor is the result of the bacterial digestion of elements in food coming out in sweat. The more sugars and processed foods a person eats, the stronger their smell will be. Some foods, most notably alliums (onions, garlic), some brassicas (broccoli, cabbage), eggs, and many spices (turmeric, cumin, capsicum) contain sulphur, which is released during bacterial digestion. Seafood can cause a person to smell fishy, but the largest natural culprits of body odor are milk and cheese, which create a very sour smell on the skin after digestion. Diets containing these foods will cause a person to "smell dirty" more often than diets without them.

Of course, if everyone is eating the same things and smelling the same way, no one will notice unless they come from somewhere else. Thus, all the accounts by early merchants and travelers referring to the odor of the people they visited. It may be apocryphal, but it is said that the Chinese who encountered Marco Polo complained that he smelled of rotten milk, and accounts from colonial ventures report that the natives often complained of their smell. This is why immigrant neighborhoods smell different—the people there are eating different foods. Don't worry though: You smell as strange to them as they do to you.

This is to say that "clean" is a relative concept, and hygiene is hardly a new idea. Soap has been around longer than humans. So, too, have many of the plants that will clean grime and oil from skin, clothes, and tools. The sea and cleansing springs have likewise been here much longer than we have.

We moderns did not come up with soap. We're actually rather late to the party. Soap is timeless, something that reminds us that time is never linear, never a march from "primitive" to "progress." Soap has always been with us, and longer still.

In Defense of Difference

I.

The country where I live, Luxembourg, is a peculiar and rare place. With a population of just over 600,000 and an area smaller than the US state of Rhode Island, it's really quite tiny. From the village in which I live, I can cycle to Germany or France in about an hour (I can see German windmills over the Moselle from a hill some 500 meters from my home). If I wanted to go to Belgium instead, it's just a two-hour bike ride away.

Luxembourg is surrounded by three larger and more populous nations (Germany has 83 million people, France has 67 million, and Belgium has 11 and a half million). The largest geographical region it occupies, the Ardennes, is primarily in Belgium, while its other region, the Moselle Valley, is generally associated with France and Germany. Although it has its own language—Lëtzebuergesch—Luxembourg's government documents are written in, and most commerce takes place in, French.

There are two rather bizarre aspects of Luxembourg's population demographics: Only 51% of its inhabitants are ancestrally Lëtzebuerger, and the number of people in the country increases by 33% during business hours. Many people commute into Luxembourg to take advantage of the higher wages (the minimum wage here is 30% higher).

The question of nationality has a lot to do with capitalism's need for an enduring, and large, underclass. As native Lëtzebuerger citizens became more educated and began working in non-manual occupations, the capitalist class encouraged mass immigration of the economically ruined Portuguese (from Portugal itself or its colonies such as Cape Verde) during Salazar's authoritarian rule there. Entire villages in Portugal are said to have been abandoned for Luxembourg, by their inhabitants, and 16% of the people here have Portuguese origins.

One might think it difficult to pinpoint what makes Luxembourg culturally distinct from the countries it borders, or what makes Lëtzebuerger people different from their neighbors and co-citizens. But when you're living here as an outsider, married to a Lëtzebuerger and living in a Lëtzebuerger village, the distinctions are sharp and obvious.

Some of my American readers—especially those who have not lived outside the borders of that sprawling nation for any period of time, and/or who consider themselves progressive— might consider it heresy at best (or potentially racist) to claim that generalizations can accurately describe a group of people. That perspective, I'd argue, reflects the exceptionalist situation of the United States (a country where very few claim ancestral ties older than 300 years) and its geographical isolation rather than a universal political truth.

II.

A conversation that my husband and I had with someone in Slovenia may help illustrate the deep differences in cultural frameworks that under-gird this problem. Our interlocutor laughed at something my husband said regarding his perception of the Balkans, and suddenly the three of us were comparing our culturally-distinct understandings of what comprised that territory. For my husband and me, the Balkans included everything that was once part of the former Yugoslavia. For the Slovenian, the Balkans also included parts of Hungary, Bulgaria, and all of Greece, though he was clear that many would not agree.

Another, much more famous Slovenian, sadly not present for that conversation, has written about this definitional problem:

> It is as if one can never receive a definitive answer to the question, "Where does it begin?" For Serbs, it begins down there in Kosovo or Bosnia, and they defend the Christian civilization against this Europe's Other. For Croats, it begins with the Orthodox, despotic, Byzantine Serbia, against which Croatia defends the values of democratic Western civilization. For Slovenes, it begins with Croatia, and we Slovenes are the last outpost of the peaceful Mitteleuropa. For Italians and Austrians, it begins with Slovenia, where the reign of the Slavic hordes starts. For Germans, Austria itself, on account of its historic connections, is already tainted by the Balkanic corruption and inefficiency. For some arrogant Frenchmen, Germany is associated with the Balkanian Eastern savagery—up to the extreme case of some conservative anti-European-Union Englishmen for whom, in an implicit way, it is ultimately the whole of continental Europe itself that functions as a kind of Balkan Turkish global empire with Brussels as the new Constantinople, the capricious despotic center threatening English freedom and sovereignty. So Balkan is always the Other: it lies somewhere else, always a little bit more to the southeast, with the paradox that, when we reach the very bottom of the Balkan peninsula, we again magically escape Balkan. Greece is no longer Balkan proper, but the cradle of our Western civilization.
>
> —Slavoj Žižek

The same conceptual difference came up as we expanded our conversation to discuss the boundaries of Europe. For my husband, who came of age during the strongest and headiest days of the European Union, the core of Europe is made up of the first 12 member nations of the EU, and each nation subsequently added expands Europe. For the Slovenian, Europe and the Balkans are entirely distinct, and he pointed to the non-contiguous situation of Greece (an original part of the EU but bordering no other EU country until 2004) to explain why Greece is actually part of the Balkans, not of Europe.

Having lived the majority of my life in the United States, this was deeply fascinating to me. Mine may not be the dominant American view, but I've always considered everything on the European continent (a funny concept, since there is no physical boundary between the land mass considered Europe and the one considered Asia) to be Europe. That includes Russia, an idea that would mortify Ukrainian nationalists who argue that they are the true frontier between Europe and Asia. I'd also include Turkey in that geographical region, an idea which would infuriate both right-wing Europeans and Turkish nationalists. Other Americans I've talked to draw the boundaries elsewhere, often talking about "Western" Europe and excluding everything east of Germany except Poland.

Such divergent conceptions may sound absurd to Americans for whom "North America" includes only three countries. Of course, many consider that there are actually twenty-three different sovereign nations in North America (twenty of which are in the Caribbean). Some would say thirty countries in total (since Central America isn't its own continent) and in some calculations there are only two, with Mexico considered part of Central America.

The implication here should be obvious: Drawing borders between one set of people and another creates deep political and cultural problems. For people in the United States—the vast majority of whom share the historical situation of being from somewhere else and the linguistic situation of dominance by one singular language—the idea of making distinctions between groups of people can seem both archaic and politically dangerous. Distinctions occur nevertheless, but they follow political fictions such as race—in which people with ancestral origins on one continent (Europe) are seen as a coherent group distinguishable from those from other continents (Asia or Africa).

This leads to many other problems. For instance, the conception of what constitutes a "white" person in the United States is completely inapplicable to Europe. Slavic peoples, Celtic peoples, and Germanic peoples don't see themselves as part of the same racial group, and in some cases their differences are as stark as those between Africans and Asians. Consider that Turks and many North African peoples would be considered white or Arab in the United States, while they may see themselves as neither white nor Arab but as a belonging to different people groups altogether.

In Europe, these differences tend to matter much more than Americans might think, but it isn't because Europe is more racist than the United States. In fact, these distinctions have very little to do with race at all, but rather with the older conceptions of what constitutes a distinct people that race theory attempted to replace. These conceptions cannot be universalized, since they are based on relative perspectives between groups in physical interaction with each other.

III.

This can be seen quite well in Luxembourg, a country that has had a relatively stable population, with few mass displacements or population influxes, for most of a millennium. Lëtzebuerger people are primarily descended from the Franks who settled here during several waves of migrations. Other Franks continued into Gaul, which is now named after them (France).

The Franks intermixed relatively peacefully with the indigenous Celtic peoples (the Treveri) but displaced the indigenous language and assimilated indigenous religious beliefs into their own—the goddess Arduinna became Freya, for example. After the Franks settled here the population remained relatively stable, particularly because of the remote and easily defensible nature of the geography. The city after which the entire country is named, Luxembourg, is one of Europe's oldest continuously inhabited fortress cities, and through deft political maneuvering Luxembourg was able to keep much of its cultural sovereignty intact during times of foreign reign.

The language itself is a strange one, because it was able to develop independently from larger language groups. This is rarely understood in the United States, but many indigenous languages persist, even in seemingly mono-lingual nations like France and Germany. France has at least five distinct, native competitors to the French language, for instance, including Alsatian, which shares a similar history with Lëtzebuergesch. Both languages are descendants of early Frankish German, which is distinct from the German spoken in Germany. Dutch has its roots in a different earlier Frankish migration, and the roots of English come from Germanic migrations to Britain.

The isolation of the people here allowed their language to develop independently (though it has a lot of French loan words), and so cultural forms and genetic patterns also developed independently. The former can be seen in several unique religious traditions, carried into Catholicism, that are uniquely Lëtzebuerger, while the latter is seen in certain physical features. Those of primarily Lëtzebuerger stock tend to have big, round heads and squat frames and appear distinct, much like Bretons in isolated villages in France who tend to be very short with almost dwarfish facial features.

To speak of such physical differences may seem problematic to the American mind, but I urge you to remember that race theory is an attempt to apply Enlightenment and Age of Reason foolishness to real cultural and historical differences. The difference between the appearance and language (there are several distinct dialects of Lëtzebuergesch) of people in this village and those in a village an hour's bike ride to the north has nothing to do with race, and everything to do with their respective historical and geographical situations.

Further complicating this discussion is our fraught relationship with the idea of generalization. A generalization is not a statement about universal truth, but a shorthand we humans use to exist in the world. A person can say "trees have leaves" without being wrong, despite the fact that some trees have needles instead, and that some trees, in the winter (and those that are dead) have no leaves at all. Asserting that trees have leaves isn't an attempt to inscribe an ideological perspective upon the world. We are usually aware of exceptions when we generalize, and we are rarely talking about universals.

Also at play is the matter of difference and comparison. The aforementioned big, round heads and squat bodies only can be said to be big, round, or squat in comparison to others. The Portuguese here don't generally have big, round heads, nor are they particularly squat in stature. The French and Germans living very close by don't share these features, and neither does my Lëtzebuerger husband, whose Dutch father's genes make his body look much less like those of his mother's relatives and ancestors.

IV.

Most importantly, such generalizations aren't political observations. There is nothing politically important about some people having big, round heads and being squat, any more than there is real political import when some people have darker skin than others. Even the most right-wing local political party makes nothing of these physical or historical differences, focusing instead on cultural and linguistic distinctions.

Right-wing local politicians see the primary threat to Lëtzebuerger cultural distinction as coming from the French, and they're not wrong. French is the primary language of commerce here and often the default language of other social interactions as well. It's rare to hear any other language spoken in a restaurant, bar, or grocery store, and French is the first language that immigrants learn in order to integrate here. Lëtzebuergesch is still spoken at home by many, and is the first language many learn, but the only real protection (and a very innocuous one at that) for Lëtzebuergesch was pushed through by the far-right party: To become a citizen, you must learn to speak and understand the language at a rudimentary level. There are no racial or cultural restrictions, only linguistic, and you need never use the language again after passing the language exam, since all official documents are written in French, German and, increasingly, in English.

The local relationship to the French is also complicated by the mass of French workers who drive into Luxembourg every day. France's economy has been a mess for a very long time, and the decay of its infrastructure is on a par with similar decay in the United States. The moment you cross the border from Luxembourg into France, by car, the highways are covered in litter, the bridges are smeared with graffiti, and the roads are in deep disrepair. I lived in France for four years and assumed that all European roadsides and cities were full of litter. When I moved to Luxembourg, I understood that I'd been wrong.

To make a universal statement about the French based on this one observation would be wrong, just as it would be to assert that all French people are assholes like those in Paris. Despite the joke I've heard here quite often—that God made France to show humans what heaven is like, but filled it with French people to show what hell is like—there isn't really a lot of bias against the French themselves.

What can be said, then? The same thing we can say about other groups: They are influenced by shared historical situations and cultural forms, and we can generalize based on our observations but never universalize.

I ride a bicycle here, daily, and the path from my small village to the village where my gym and grocery store are follows a route used by German workers. The road is very rural and very beautiful, but often quite deadly to animals and even humans because people drive absurdly fast. Whenever I hear a car speeding along the path, well before I actually see the vehicle, I get off the road as quickly as possible to avoid the fate suffered by my cat, my neighbor's cat, several deer, a fox, and several humans.

Every time I encounter such a car, I look at the license plate and note that they are always German. What does that say about Germans? Nothing universal. But general observations can be made. This route is used by German workers. Speeding incidents tend to happen most often in late afternoon, right about the time those workers are leaving for home. They don't live here, and so don't have a sense of direct connection to this place. They are likely in a hurry to get home after work, as most people are. And they live in a country where speed limits rarely exist on highways and driving insanely fast is acceptable behavior.

A similar generalization can be made about Belgians, based on observation and derived from understandings about their national situation. While my husband drove us home from our honeymoon, we got stuck in a traffic jam on a French highway north of Strasbourg. Many cars were attempting to maneuver past the rest of the vehicles to get ahead of the blockage, and a group of 30 motorcyclists pushed their way through the gap between the two lanes of slowed cars. Every single one of the motorcycles and maneuvering cars had a Belgian license plate.

Which could be seen as mere co-incidence, or as an opportunity to assert that all Belgians are assholes. A more interesting generalization, however, arises when you know about the shoddy state of Belgian highways and the complete unreliability of Belgian highway markings and signs. To avoid getting stuck traveling in the wrong direction in Belgium (something that happened to my husband and I multiple times near Liège), you often have to make illegal turns and other maneuvers, and everyone else is doing the same thing. If you are accustomed to driving like that, you probably find yourself driving that way outside of Belgium as well.

There is a usefulness to generalization and cultural analysis that has been overlooked by many progressive, liberal, and left frameworks. Completely rejecting generalization, or conflating generalization with universalizing, makes it impossible to talk about actual human differences without resorting to meaningless abstractions like "structures" and "systems." Race theory is a universalization that must be avoided (in both its right-wing and social justice forms) because race is a ridiculous and baseless grand narrative that attempts not only to universalize differences, but to impose them.

The reduction or destruction of difference is just as pernicious as race theory, something that, until about ten years ago, the left still understood. Globalization flattens differences by imposing singular forms across cultures and people groups. The general trend of capitalism is toward universalization: everywhere the same crops, the same products, the same brands and corporations, the same languages, the same beliefs, the same political frameworks, the same currencies.

It is tragic, but not inevitable, that resistance to the destruction of cultural difference is now primarily the purview of nationalist and right-wing frameworks. We all lose when cultural differences are flattened and subsumed into capitalist imperial forms, and when people are categorized according to newly constructed identities divorced from cultural and historical situations. We all lose when languages, and the ways of thinking they embody, disappear. Even in the case of cultural differences that we don't like, and that cause conflict, we all lose when they are replaced by bland and passive consumption of global media production.

Greener Grass

I was very sad recently, and then I wasn't sad anymore. It's a long story. My life here is amazing, relentlessly gorgeous, and really engaging. But I am very far away from everything and almost everyone I knew, for most of my life, and sometimes things seem so strange, so foreign, so different that I get overwhelmed.

Several months ago, a self-styled social justice activist called me out on social media. I saved the "call out" and looked at it often, until I finally deleted it. This person, who has never met me, was angry about something I'd written that had become very popular. The "call out" said I was a "working-class version of a trust-fund baby," living in Europe as a "leftist version of a sovereign citizen," and so no one should read anything I write.

I saved that "call out" because it was so extreme, and so dazzlingly contradictory (what's a working-class version of a trust fund baby?) From what I've been able to learn about this person's life, they've made much more money than I ever have, but they still wallow in frustration and despair, spending hours on social media preaching an empty dogma that only makes sense on Facebook. They're one of those sorts who are fully defined by their opinions, and see everything through the lens of oppression.

I also saved it because it gave me a sense of what people who don't like me think that my life is like and, as skewed as it is, it's good to have that reflection. I mean, "leftist version of a sovereign citizen" actually sounds pretty cool. Like I'm a hacker evading border controls and police raids, or an old-school Catalonian anarchist guiding people over the Pyrenees.

If anything, it sounds like a beautiful fantasy. I've heard other such fantasies. I've been accused of being a communist infiltrator into pagan spaces, and a mastermind manipulator who has minions and thralls willing to do my bidding. There's even someone who believes I hexed them and that's why they are now addicted to drugs.

We give other people so much power, huh? They're all living on greener pastures than we ever will.

My sadness ended when I went to visit some friends of mine, neighbors I hadn't seen for a long time. Last year I spent hours with them, because they pasture near my grove, a fallen tree next to a circle of alders through which runs a stream. I go there to think, to talk, to cry, to laugh, sometimes to lay unclothed in the sun, sometimes to do what people might call magic (but I just call "talking"), and mostly just to be.

There are seven of them this year. Last year there were only three. They come running when they see me, stand in a circle around me, or sometimes in a line. They eat grass from my hands, and sometimes apples, and mostly they tell me things.

These friends are massive Clydesdale horses, all muscle. I went, with my family and partner, to visit them today, and they came running at me so hard that my youngest nephew got scared. We gave them apples, and one stole an ear of corn from my other nephew's pocket. He had "stolen" that ear of corn from a field himself, so it was all fair play. On the way to their pasture, we ate blackberries and plums and wood sorrel, trudged through mud and nettle, talked to cows, and waved hello to deer. Then we finally saw the horses, who came running.

One of the most widely venerated goddesses in pre-Christian Europe wasn't a Roman deity at all, but a Gallic one: Epona. A goddess of horses, later adopted into imperial religion as a goddess of cavalry, she really only cares about the horses. Be good to horses and she may have something to say to you. Be unkind to them and she will definitely have something to say.

They are such brilliant beasts, really, and so deeply kind. When I visited them but had no apples, I used my hands to pull up clumps of grass for them, "better" grass from beyond a barbed wire fence where their muzzles could not reach. Greener on the other side.

Epona was adopted into imperial Roman religion the same way that faith, folk belief, and human life itself was assimilated first into Christianity and then into capitalism. Epona is a goddess of horses, not horsemen. Turned into the goddess of those who use and control the being that she is actually the goddess of, Epona became a political tool.

Fortunately, there are still horses, and Epona still exists as well, though few speak to either of them these days. My life is mostly about speaking to them, and all the other thems to whom no one speaks much anymore. The trees around here get an earful, I assure you. The streams get an occasional "hello" whenever I cross them. The ravens get an answer to their calls, but I make an effort to ignore the magpies because honestly, they talk too much.

I sometimes feel very far away from everything I knew, but then I reconsider. I knew crows, and trees, and streams. Different ones, yes, but you can talk to them all the same way. I knew people there, and though I know fewer here, they speak with the same human voices as the people I knew.

There are fewer people here, but more horses. The gods are a little more talkative here, too, though I don't know if that's because there are fewer humans to drown out their voices or if I've just learned to listen better. Perhaps both.

What I've wanted to say to that "social justice activist" who has fantasies about what I'm doing with my life is that you can just let yourself be instead. Social media makes everyone's life look more fantastic than your own, but the problem doesn't lie with them, or even with your perception of them: The problem is your perception of yourself.

You can go talk to horses, you know, and maybe even to Epona, if she'll listen. You can talk to ravens and trees and streams, and you don't need to do it the way I did. You don't have to give up everything you know, leave the security and safety of your life behind and travel practically moneyless in a foreign land until you find a place that feels like home. Instead, you can just turn off your phone, stop staring at a screen, and look at your own life and the lives of others with wonder, rather than fear and resentment.

Everything isn't some epic political struggle into which you must constantly throw all your diminishing effort. You can just go feed apples to some horses or throw some unsalted peanuts to some crows. You can sit down near a stream, and just be.

Sure, sometimes the grass is greener on the other side. But you have hands: You can pull some of that green grass up and pass it through the barbed wire fence so that the horses on the other side can reach it.

The Demon and the Genius

Until just a few hundred years ago, it was a rare to find religious or cultural frameworks that believed spirits have no influence on peoples' lives. Only since the Protestant Reformation, and the subsequent obsession with "reason," have Europeans stopped believing such a thing. And I can still walk through my village in this modern, secular, capitalist nation and find plenty of people who believe spirits exist and interact with us.

Those people might disagree about what constitutes a spirit, or might call them ghosts, angels, or demons instead. In Christianity, angels are a particular category of spirits. Demons are of the same order of being as angels, but represent a different genre or state (fallen) within that order. Saints, I'd argue, are likewise a kind of spirit, though I don't think the village priest would describe them that way. But saints reportedly appear to people as signs or in some sort of spiritual body, similar to the way angels and demons do.

Even within Christianity, whether a spirit is classified as an angel, a demon, or a saint is often quite relative. Consider Joan of Arc, who claimed that St. Catherine, St. Margaret, and St. Michael (the angel) spoke to her, urging her to fight against the English and evict them from France. Her English interrogators were not so convinced, asserting that she was a witch and communicating with demons, not with angels and saints.

It's worth noting that the question of spirit communication itself wasn't up for debate. Both the devout English and the devout French readily accepted that she was speaking to *someone*, because her intense charisma and the supernatural nature of her victories were neither one in question. What was questionable, however, was precisely who was giving her such power. Because the English saw the results of her work as evil and malevolent, they believed her powers must be infernal. For the French, finding themselves free of English rule, Joan of Arc was guided by God and his emissaries.

This is hardly an unusual debate. The slaves in Haiti who made a pact with the Loa in exchange for victory against their French masters were either engaging in a satanic rite or a ritual agreement with kindly spirits, a difference of opinion coming down to whether you were one of the masters or one of the slaves.

II.

I went to the gym a few days ago, for the first time in over three months. I'm not sure exactly why I stopped going. Lots of things happened. I got married, and I was working on a book, and I went on a honeymoon, and then I injured my foot, and I was generally busy, but none of those are reasons not to go to the gym. They're just excuses I made after the fact. It was around the time of my birthday, earlier this year, that my usual four-day-a-week routine dropped off, becoming first three days, then two, then once a week for a few weeks, and then not at all.

It was really, really hard to go back. I've been haranguing myself for the last few months about not going, constantly telling myself that I'll go again, I need to go, I want to go, and there is absolutely no good reason not to go. My self-reproach was futile, and only deepened my depression about not going to the gym. Finally, this week, I worked out a way to trick myself into going again. I set up a new training appointment, and told the trainer ahead of time that I just wanted to do cardio and some light weight training.

I showed up for the appointment ready to argue with her, expecting her to plan an intense workout for me, despite my stated wishes. That's what happened. I tried arguing with her, and almost pulled the ridiculous, whining "I'm in charge here because I'm paying you" routine. But have you tried arguing with an MMA fighter? Just because she's half your size doesn't make it any easier. When a small woman who can beat you bloody in less than a minute is telling you that were already strong and that it'll take less time to get back to your baseline if you do what she says, there's no point in doing anything but listening to her.

I don't get pushed like that a lot in my life. The last person who did that for me was the tantric therapist I worked with to get over all the stifling beliefs I had about myself. We tend to have to pay people to push us now. The stern father who pushes his kids to be better than they think they are—a role I've seen taken up by mothers in some cultures (when I was young all my Puerto Rican friends had mothers who pushed them like that)—is now so rare that Jordan Peterson made millions by telling people to stop sniveling and make their beds.

Will is different from desire. We desire lots of things, and we even convince ourselves that our desires are fully our own. I fully desired to go to the gym, but I also fully desired other things, like inertia, and not to be so exhausted that all movement hurt for several days following a workout. Will is when you make a choice between desires, when you choose to shape your desires around another desire, even to forego pursuing some desires because they conflict with what you've chosen to desire most.

Having someone push you to do what you truly desire to do is rare. You usually have to search for such people, and they can be unpleasant to be around. They tend to get bored with your false hopes and dead-end fantasies, which means they get bored with your excuses about why you cannot do the thing you truly want to do.

Of course, there is a difference between being pushed to become fully who you are, and doing something because of external pressure. We don't have the language or the spiritual framework to speak about agency without slipping into responsibility on one hand and culpability on the other. Doing something because someone pressures you to do it is an abdication of agency. Being pushed to do something that is in alignment with your will means that someone is helping you ascend your own throne.

III.

The subtle difference between the two—and our cultural inability to understand that difference—explains why shame has become both a powerful weapon and a powerful defense. The core mechanism of a social media crusade is shame, with the goal being either to shame the person into obedience or to stain them so thoroughly with the dye of shame that they are forever banished from the order of cultural meaning.

At the same time, "shaming" is the term used to dismiss any attempt to apply naturalistic reasoning to problems for which there might be practical solutions. It is "fat-shaming" to suggest high rates of diabetes and obesity in the United States are linked to the consumption of certain foods rather than others, or "poor-shaming" to propose that the yearly trampling deaths at Wal-Mart and Target are a sign of an unhealthy consumerist obsession. It is mean and horrible to point out that there might be a better way of doing things, that there might be external forces and personal decisions contributing to bad situations. Doing so might make people feel bad, or ashamed, and only people who are evil or wrong should be made to feel that way.

I admit that I felt quite ashamed that I'd stopped going to the gym. There was no external reason for my feeling of shame. My husband wasn't shaming me about it, nor was "society." Going to the gym is entirely my choice, just as not going to the gym is also entirely my choice, and neither choice derives from the idea that I am "supposed to" go or that I need to conform to some standard of beauty or behavior. I had decided to go, but I wasn't going. Something was holding me back.

The roots of the words "shame" and "embarrassment," though they have different linguistic origins, share a similar secondary resonance: that of reluctance or hesitation. "Shame" is derived from a word that meant "to cover," with the sense that you might cover your face or hesitate to show yourself in public because of dishonor. "Embarrass," in its oldest sense, meant to hinder (literally "to bar"). Being embarrassed by something signified that there was something stopping you or holding you back.

These original roots were verbs, not nouns. They signified neither static nor end conditions, but rather active processes of hindrance. To be ashamed was to be in a moment of hesitation, to be embarrassed was to be in a moment of holding yourself (or being held) back.

So, by being ashamed of not going to the gym, and being embarrassed about it, I was aware that I was in a process of active hesitation and hindrance. To put it more crudely, I was suffering a constipation of the will, a moment of blockage. No one else was hindering me, and I could not figure out how to stop hindering myself.

Looking at the way shame operates in social media crusades, it should be obvious that the intention is to hinder others, to bar them, to make them reluctant to show themselves. Successful crusades crush the will of the target, succeeding only when the victim actively hinders themself as well.

Having once been very overweight, and also having once been very poor, I can tell you that there's lot of shame in both conditions. You don't want to be either of those things. You don't really know how to get out of those conditions, and you can't easily discern between the external and the internal forces that are hindering you. Thus, when someone tells you that you shouldn't be fighting other poor people for goods manufactured by poor people a continent away, or that the food you are eating isn't good for your body or your health, it's not the easiest thing to hear.

Regardless, you need to hear such things, and such things need to be said. Those words aren't shaming, rather they illuminate the shame (hindrance) that you are already experiencing and, like the stern father, my really aggressive MMA-fighting gym trainer, or a spirit or god, they try to help you stop hindering yourself.

IV.

I wrote earlier that I don't know why I didn't go back to the gym for so long, but that's not actually true. I didn't want to. I told myself that I did, but I didn't. Working out is really hard, honestly, and kind of awful, even as it's also brilliant and life affirming, and feels incredible.

Sometimes I don't want to do hard things. I think that's probably true for everyone. Sometimes we'd rather do easier things, or nothing at all, and sometimes we should. Unfortunately, we also want more from our lives, want better circumstances and conditions, want to feel better and more alive than we currently feel. And it's precisely in that space of contradiction that what we call shame arises.

In other words, we become aware of our conflicting desires, and our struggle to sort them. We realize that we are hindered, reluctant, hesitating, holding back and hiding our faces because we cannot find our agency and cannot manifest our will.

The Greek concept of the *eudaemon* and the Roman concept of the *genius* are useful here, perhaps more so than the modern psychological concepts that we use to talk about will and agency. The *eudaemon* of the Greeks was seen as a kind of friendly, intelligent spirit bound in some way to an individual, a bit like the way Christians conceived of the "guardian angel." The *genius* of the Romans was somewhat similar, though it was understood to be intrinsic to the person.

Both the Romans and the Greeks were animist peoples, believing themselves to share a world teeming with spirits. Each culture conceived of those spirits and their relationship to them differently, but their frameworks share enough core features that the differences matter less than the similarities. For the Greeks, *daemons* could be helpful and benevolent (the *agathodaemons* or the *eudaemons*), unhelpful and malevolent (the *kakodaemons*), or neutral. The Roman understanding of spirits was similar, though their spirits (*genii*) were an inhabiting presence. For instance, a place had a *genius* (the *genius loci*) just as a person had one, and some *genii* could become so significant as to be seen as lesser deities.

These Greek and Roman concepts have a lot in common with the beliefs of other animist peoples in tutelary spirits, ancestors, and totems, but particularly relevant to this discussion are the continuations of these frameworks into Christianity. The idea of the "guardian angel" is the most obvious such continuation, one that was iterated early in Church history, codified in the 12th century, and remains official and active Catholic doctrine today. Reference Pope Francis' discussion of guardian angels during a Mass four years ago:

> There is the danger of not going on the journey. And how many people settle down, and don't set out on the journey, and their whole life is stalled, without moving, without doing anything... It is a danger. Like that man in the Gospel who was afraid to invest the talent. He buried it, and [said] "I am at peace, I am calm. I can't make a mistake. So I won't take a risk." And so many people don't know how to make the journey, or are afraid of taking risks, and they are stalled. But we know that the rule is that those who are stalled in life end up corrupted... The angels help us, they push us to continue on the journey...
>
> ...The angel is authoritative; he has authority to guide us. Listen to him. "Hearken to his voice, and do not rebel against him." Listen to the inspirations, which are always from the Holy Spirit – but the angel inspires them. But I want to ask you a question: Do you speak with your angel? Do you know the name of your angel? Do you listen to your angel? Do you allow yourself to be led by hand along the path, or do you need to be pushed to move?
>
> ...Our angel is not only with us; he also sees God the Father. He is in relationship with Him. He is the daily bridge, from the moment we arise to the moment we go to bed. He accompanies us and is a link between us and God the Father. The angel is the daily gateway to transcendence, to the encounter with the Father: that is, the angel helps me to go forward because he looks upon the Father, and he knows the way. Let us not forget these companions along the journey.

Setting aside for a moment the references to "God the Father" and the "Holy Spirit," Pope Francis's explanation of the role of the angels is fully in line with the ancient pagan understandings of both the *eudaemon* and the *genius*. Flashes of inspiration or insight (of "genius") were attributed to these spirits, as well as intense moments of intuition about the consequences of certain choices or the motives of others (like when you know you are being lied to). Plato has Socrates thank his *eudaemon* for helping him avoid attempts on his life, as well as for giving him insight into the nature of others' questions.

Although we set it aside for a moment, even the language of "God the Father" and the "Holy Spirit" are in line with pagan understanding, since it was through a person's genius or eudaemon that they interacted with the rest of the divine world (manifested as other *genii* or spirits). Everything had a spirit or, more correctly, everything interacted with everything else as spirit because everything has and is a spirit.

For the Romans and the Greeks, the *genius* and the *eudaemon* could also be called a person's "true will" or "destiny" because of their ability to see what was best for a person. These spirits helped people to become better, to gain more wealth or renown, to survive or avoid harmful situations, and they also provided insight into the likely consequences of actions and the emotions of others. Thus, the general goal or work of these spirits was to help you to become what we might call the "best version" of yourself.

The moments of hindrance and reluctance described by the words "shame" and "embarrassment" can best be seen as moments of disconnection from the *genius* and the *eudaemon*. I've heard Christians describe this kind of disconnection as a sense of being "out of a state of grace," or of "backsliding." One of the functions or roles of the genius was to act as a conduit, intermediary, or translator between the person and the divine. In some witchcraft traditions, the genius is called "the god-self" or the "god-soul," and it is seen as separate from (and often in conflict with) the mind, but close kin with the animal or bodily self. This perspective parallels (or is informed by) older shamanic views on the matter of humans having multiple souls, one of which can interact with other souls independent of the body-soul.

V.

The Roman concept of the *genius* and the Greek concept of the *eudaemon*, which tended to fold into each other, were split apart by Christian doctrine. Augustine made this break, translating the *genius* as the "soul" and the *eudaemon* as a "guardian angel." The Church also stripped all non-human beings of their *genii*, breaking Christianity off from the pagan animist cultures that mothered it. Christianity attempted to simplify the relationship between the human and the divine into a two-party interaction: There was only the human soul and the divine one-god, and only spirits in the service of that one-god (the angels) and *genii* of those who were faithful to him (the saints) could speak on his behalf.

In Christianity today, angels have counterparts that still bear the older Greek name: the demons. The demons of Christianity are the Greek *kakodaemon*, the class of malevolent spirits who desire to harm humanity. The Church didn't come up with the idea of such beings, nor with ways of dealing with them. It's a core feature of animist frameworks that some spirits are just not nice, and rites and rituals of exorcism far predate the birth of Jesus.

Though we've generally discarded the ideas of good and evil in secular modernity, we preserve the concept that a malevolence can possess a person and manifest itself in their behavior. As the author of one essay on demons wrote, "...in a vestigial echo of the truth, we sometimes say 'he is wrestling with his demons' when such battles are particularly dramatic." There are many such vestigial echoes, including when we speak of someone being "possessed" or "gripped" by an idea, mood, fear, or passion.

It is subtle yet profound, I think, that when someone is not acting normal we ask them "what's gotten into you?" And that we speak of something "coming over," "come onto," or "taking hold of" a person.

We can now return to the matter of shame and embarrassment by way of Pope Francis's mass, and a peculiar point he makes regarding hesitation and stagnation:

> And how many people settle down, and don't set out on the journey, and their whole life is stalled, without moving, without doing anything... It is a danger....and so many people don't know how to make the journey, or are afraid of taking risks, and they are stalled. But we know that the rule is that those who are stalled in life end up corrupted...

Shame and embarrassment are both active states of hesitation, of holding oneself back from action. Being in such a state can lead to long periods of inaction, of being "stalled in life," which Francis asserts leads to becoming corrupted.

Much of my work these last few years has been trying to understand the psychological state of *ressentiment* and how it influences mass politics. *Ressentiment* says "I am not happy; therefore you are not allowed to be happy." As Kierkegaard notes, *ressentiment* ultimately says, "I cannot act and therefore you shall not be allowed to act." The "wet blanket" or "stick in the mud" state of the person in *ressentiment* is physical: The fire of life has gone out of them, and they actively seek to douse the fires of others.

Shame and embarrassment are key here. Prolonged states of inaction and hesitation (constipation of the will) only increase that feeling of shame until something is done. That something might be good and helpful (finally going back to the gym), or it might be harmful and malevolent (acts of suicide or abuse). The latter is the route of ressentiment, which seeks to replicate itself in others, to make the whole world hesitate, out of fear, and abdicate their agency.

Ressentiment seems to me best described as a spirit. It is the corruption, of which Pope Francis speaks, that comes upon a person who is stalled, who hesitates, who does not risk, and who no longer understands that they've chosen that situation themself. The "angels" who help "push us" were, for the Greeks, the *eudaemon*, helpful demons. For the Romans, that helper was the actual spirit of the person, assigned to them at birth and accompanying them to the grave. We might now call this spirit our "will" or "agency," but it's really the same thing.

Can we call *ressentiment* a demon? Yes, I think we can, if we use the Greek framework and call it a *kakodaemon*. Some demons want to help humans, some demons want to destroy humans. As I've said before, "there are gods who do not care how this ends, only that it does."

The spirit of *ressentiment* is malevolent, and its goal seems to be the destruction of the genius, in both the Roman and the modern usage of the word. The person who shines too bright, who ventures too far, who builds too well or creates too beautifully is a genius because he or she has a particularly profound *genius*. Their spirits are strong, bright, glorious, and they inspire (raise the spirits of, enspirit) others.

VI.

The goal of a social media crusade is to crush a spirit, to force a person to cover or hide themselves in shame, to bar themselves from action because of embarrassment. Such crusades pre-date the Woke and the internet that birthed them. We've always had bullies, "mean girls," and communal or mass acts of shaming and terror. While we can debate, endlessly, the causes of such campaigns, what's more interesting is the predictable impact on their victims.

It's become a trope in the stories of mass shooters, the fact that he (usually he) was socially awkward, ostracized, and bullied. The typical response is to remind ourselves (and others) that there are plenty of people who are bullied but do not become mass killers. This is disingenuous. Plenty of people drive drunk but do not get into car accidents, and yet we all agree that alcohol's effect on a driver is dangerous.

If there's any modern event that we can all agree upon as being demonic (in the Christian sense) or kakodaemonic (in the Greek sense), it would be a mass shooting. We spend days, weeks, months trying to understand what could possibly possess a person to blow out the brains of schoolchildren or to murder groups of strangers at a shopping mall, a picnic, or a church. No explanation ever feels sufficient.

Demons offer a very sufficient explanation, from within the framework of animism. By "demons," then, I mean demons not as the counterpart to angels, rather demons as spirits, some of whom are nice and helpful, many of whom are indifferent (but might be persuadable in either direction), some who are mischievous or harsh, and many that are malevolent and wish to see humans suffer, die, and even disappear completely from the world which we share with them.

Christianity is not the first religious system to create rites or rituals of exorcism. In fact, on the world stage, it could fairly be said to have come late to this party. The role of the priest-figure (shaman, mystic, etc.) in animist religions is to be an intermediary between humans and spirits, including placating and sometimes banishing, fighting off, or exorcising spirits that are unwelcome or unhelpful. In our modern world we have psychologists and psychiatrists, those who study the psyche (which means "soul" in Greek) to diagnose its disorders and put it back into order. But they cannot tell us what comes upon a person, what possesses them.

Christianity formalized exorcism rituals and created a moral code for people to follow to protect themselves from the social and soul conditions that might lead to possession. Renaissance grimoires invoke Christ and the angels to help bind demons to the magician's will: It's an efficient framework, and one that works. But it works the way Starbucks works if you want a coffee or McDonald's works if you want a hamburger. There is no nuance. There is no customization. Mass-produced, convenience goods will not save our souls.

In the Christian framework, Joan of Arc was either a saint or a witch while, from an animist perspective, she was both. She could interact with spirits (angels and saints), retain her sanity and her seat, and translate messages from those spirits into massive cultural and political change. Her *genius* shone brightly enough to convince others of the rightness of her cause, and spirits (the *eudaemon*) warned her of danger and informed her of the motives of her enemies. These abilities and relationships are the traits of a holy person—a saint—and also of a witch. Both the French who followed her and the English who executed her were correct.

A Christian demonology cannot hold this paradox. We need a deeper ecology of demons. What leads a person to become possessed by malevolent spirits, and how do we prevent it? How might such spirits be placated? What is the goal of the spirits that overcome a person in addiction or in suicide? And, if we turn our attention to the matter of *ressentiment* and other mass "psychoses," is there a larger presence behind such manifestations?

We need an ecology of demons in relation to the genius (in both senses of the word.) Peter Grey's *The Two Antichrists* is a good albeit indirect beginning toward an ecology of the genius in the modern sense. The technocratic "space" order, including NASA and SpaceX, was born from the demon-soaked obsessions of occultist Jack Parsons and inspired by the literary pulp fantasies of raving mad men who believed they were in contact with alien or demonic intelligences. To put it bluntly, The Machine is the work of demons.

In his book, *Ani.Mystic*, Gordon White points out that indigenous animist cultures have always attributed their knowledge, their wisdom, their flashes of insight, and especially their technology to spirit-teachers. Spirits of plants teach humans how to be in relationship with the plant; ancestors come to descendants in dreams to warn of danger or to push for action. Spirits of stars and gods gifted us new ways of boatbuilding, of timekeeping, and even of governance. Christianity and Islam also have star-spirits as a central part of their founding narratives: Muslims turn toward a fallen meteor five times a day to pray and the magi followed a star to the birth of Jesus.

Cultures that believe in spirits and spirit guidance have ways of determining which spirits give good advice, and what their motives are. We don't apply that kind of discernment now, and so technologies are produced, sold widely, and allowed to transform the world merely because they're new. Which demons pushed humans to create the internet, and what were they hoping to accomplish? Which spirits sent the dreams that inspired factories, or penicillin, or nuclear fission, or the printing press? And perhaps the more urgent question—what were they on about?

If we allow ourselves to believe, again, in spirits, we might have an easier time understanding the political problems sweeping through our societies—particularly the increasing impact of mass *ressentiment*—because that framework poses questions we don't currently allow ourselves to ask. If *ressentiment* is a spirit (a *kakodaemon*), then what's its goal and how did it seize some of us so thoroughly? How do we exorcise it, and how do we help people avoid its dark influence?

This framework doesn't conflict with Marxist materialism. The best way to keep someone from becoming miserable and trying to spread their misery to others is to make sure they've got the means to live a satisfied life. If people are not starving, if they've got dignified and meaningful work, if their village hasn't been bombed by drone airstrikes and their children haven't been poisoned by radiation or chemicals in their food or water, they're much less likely to want to similarly ravage the lives of others. If someone is not sitting at a computer all day eating trash food while reading that the cis-hetero-patriarchy or the global Jewish cabal is the source of all their problems, they might not try to impose their own bodily alienation onto the rest of society. It doesn't even really conflict with the Christian framework, provided we keep in mind that one person's saint is another person's witch, and that neither position actually contradicts the other.

Ressentiment is, I think, the best place to start, because it's breeding violence everywhere. If shame and embarrassment are really the key to *ressentiment* (and I think they are), we must come up with ways to help people stop holding themselves back, stop self-hindering, and to teach them—from whichever framework we use—how to know what they truly desire.

The Imaginal Gate

Because of my very poor and extremely insecure childhood, and its effects on my body and sense of self, "losing" myself in something—more accurately, "hiding"—became my go-to mechanism to escape the terror of my material conditions. I hid in books especially. In books I could live multiple, entirely different lives when my own life felt unlivable.

Escaping into books isn't a bad habit, compared to other habits I could have turned to like drugs or alcohol. I used both, for a little bit in my early 20s, but never to the extent that I used reading. Work became my other escape: working too much, keeping myself too busy, and making work for myself when work was not otherwise available.

My dependence on overwork came directly from fear of poverty. Though none of my jobs pulled me out of the lowest economic tier or ended my financial precarity, working hard felt like some access to agency, something I could do.

When I was a social worker at a homeless shelter, I'd often pick up at least one overtime shift each week. These were overnight shifts, which are deeply unpleasant ways to spend a night. Working through the dark hours under garish fluorescent lights makes you lose the earth a bit, makes you feel out of sync not just with time but also with gravity. I remember thinking, after months of those nights, that the earth might forget to pull me toward it, one day, and I would be flung violently from this spinning globe into the endless abyss of space.

I really enjoy my work, these days, but I've not fully unlearned those habits. Writing and developmental editing are infinitely more satisfying than social work, or any of the other jobs I've had, but I notice that I still lose or hide myself in them. The problem is that writing is a horrible place to hide. To write well you must write from what's true and honest about yourself, which means that people read what's true and honest about you. You're hiding in the one place where everyone can easily see you.

Editing the essays for this compilation meant reading through my own writing of the last three years. It was like reading my own history, or at least my official narrative of it. The me who lived through those years, that history, was a witness too, comparing my public account to what I had not written nor ever could.

I've woven glimpses of that unwritten history into these essays, occasional references, both conscious and unconscious, to the life I actually lived rather than the life I narrated. Some careful or consistent readers may have found those bits told them more than anything I could have said directly.

Three years ago, almost to the day as I write this, I got on a train to visit my sister. It was my first trip to Luxembourg, a trip that would lead to me living here and completely changing my way of looking at the world.

I've told this story in bits and pieces elsewhere, but I'll tell it again. When I was 36—9 years ago now—I had what I thought was a schizophrenic break. I thought it was schizophrenia because my mother is schizophrenic, but my experience didn't match anything I knew about schizophrenia. I was hearing voices like my mother did, but those voices weren't destructive, like the voices she heard. In fact, they were incredibly, eerily helpful, and always insightful, despite the fact that I didn't initially understand what they meant.

At the same time, I started having intense dreams that "spilled out" into the waking world. I'd wake up utterly exhausted, or unusually refreshed, and feel as though the foreign landscapes from my dreams stayed with me throughout the day. Then something else began to happen. Always to my surprise, but decreasingly to my alarm, I'd feel myself to be "somewhere else" while also being exactly where I was.

I remember one such moment. I was walking across a university campus, taking a shortcut on the way to my job. The slant of light across the trees and a certain quality of the wind made me look around and suddenly I was walking across low grass growing in sandy soil. I smelled salt, heard waves, and saw that I was in a place I didn't know yet but would later recognize.

Such things happened frequently, but were never disruptive. I managed to keep working, and my job began to seem more purposeful and less burdensome. That job was a means to an end, I realized, but it took me a while to understand what that end was.

I remember the moment I figured out what I was about to do. It was afternoon and I was outside, writing in my journal. I wrote the words "I'm moving to Europe" without quite realizing that I was writing them. I stared dumbly at the ink, unclear why I'd inscribed those words, not even feeling that it was me who wrote them. Those words felt like a prophecy, not just an idea scrawled on paper.

I stared, read those words again, and then decided to do what they said I would do.

I found myself, later, in many of the places I saw during those odd moments of walking vision. That shoreline turned out to be near a place I once visited in Morbihan, while another landscape revealed itself just over a low mountain in Finistère. The sense of recognition and familiarity came more profoundly through scent than vision and was occasionally quite disorienting. I'd smelled these places before and I knew them again by their smell, the same way I knew my grandparents' home by the scent of the coffee they drank, and the smell of pine and oak in the forests around their home.

These were places I'd never been, but I knew them already. Everything felt burningly correct. I'd arrived at the place I knew, by smell, from dreams and visions. I'd come to the place I thought I would finally rest, and for a little while everything seemed perfect.

It wasn't, though. I began to feel that I was going to be someplace else, later. I didn't like this feeling. I'd dismantled an entire life in order to arrive somewhere, and though the place I'd arrived didn't feel entirely like the future I'd seen, I didn't want to go somewhere else again.

I got stuck. Really, really stuck. I used to have this fear—inspired by a deeply depressing stop on a cross-country train trip in the United States—of getting off at a station and forgetting to get back on before the train left. What if I could never get back on and somehow forgot I had been on my way somewhere else? I'd be trapped in a living purgatory, constantly visiting the train station. I'd watch the passengers entrain, and leave, and I'd wonder where they were going without remembering that I had meant to go there, too.

Getting "stuck" meant something specific in this case. I'd overstayed a visa because of a relationship with a man I'd not yet understood was an abuser. I had become enchanted, or rather enthralled, and the next two years of my life made all those helpful voices and mystic visions suddenly seem diabolic.

Those two years blur together into one terrible knot. There are occasional threads of memory I can tease out from it, but the entire experience was one of increasing misery, isolation, and degradation of self. Abuse does that, leads you to forget who you are and what you are capable of, and to doubt everything and everyone that might help you.

When I was able to work out my visa situation, to become "legal" again in Europe, the abuse accelerated. The day I received my regularization papers, he hit me and shouted at me for hours, and did so many more times that week. Before that day, leaving him meant leaving Europe. Now I could leave him without having to go back to the United States.

I hadn't even thought of leaving him, so degraded had my soul become. His certainty that I planned to leave made him more abusive, but the idea didn't occur to me until I visited my sister. She'd moved her family to Luxembourg for work, and now that I didn't have to worry about being caught, crossing borders, as an illegal immigrant, I could finally visit her. So I did.

I didn't tell her what he'd done or what he was really like, but she's my sister. She could see it on my face, the sorrow shaping me into a semblance of a shadow of myself. She asked and I told her, but I still didn't think of leaving him.

When I returned home, everything got worse, and then worse still. More screaming, more violence. He started breaking my things, often by throwing them at me. He'd wake me in the middle of the night to yell at me, like a living nightmare. He'd demand literal receipts for where I'd been while he was at work, timestamped grocery tickets and bus transfers. He'd go through my phone, reading texts and deleting contacts, never finding anything incriminating and so conjuring conspiracies.

Finally, I did think of leaving. *Just for a little while,* I told myself. Just to give him time to calm down and maybe get therapy or something. I even left a few important things in that place to trick myself into leaving, to assure myself that I'd come back soon, that I wasn't doing anything permanent.

I didn't go back. I got back on the train I had intended to be on, all along.

It seems so obvious now, but I could not have seen it then. I needed to live through all of that, because I needed to experience the inevitable conclusion that my former ideas about myself and the world would lead to. I needed to know the consequences of those ideas, how they created prisons for the self from which escape seemed an unthinkable idea.

The last three years of my life, and of my writing, have been the result of finally understanding all of this. Seeing how the very same ideas, patterns, and beliefs that trapped me fuel the political frameworks I criticize has been particularly difficult, as so much of my former life was devoted to those frameworks. Even harder has been watching so many people I knew and cared about entrench themselves further into those ideas the worse their personal lives get, becoming fundamentalists of identity because they don't know who they are any longer.

That still haunts me, and my writing. Reading through these essays, it's impossible not to see the reflections. I'm still trying to comprehend how I got to that point, so I can comprehend how they got to that point. Trying to understand how I finally escaped, so I can explain how they might be able to, as well.

I've tried to think and to work my way out of problems, hiding from the hard truths about my life and the world around me rather than looking at them directly.

But I only escaped by means utterly unrelated to thinking or to work.

It wasn't just the voices and the visions. If we know anything from myth and religious histories, oracles and prophecies are always ignored until the conditions they warn of finally manifest. By then, it's usually too late, and all we really learn is that we refused to learn, and will probably refuse next time, too.

I escaped when I finally stopped trying to think and work my way out of things. I had to sabotage those mechanistic parts of myself to let something fully irrational guide me, something that couldn't be explained, defined, or reasoned with.

Citing the medieval Christian and Orthodox framework, Paul Kingsnorth links the "irrational" to the Greek concept of nous, which is a good way to think of it:

> Medieval Christianity placed a high value on the intellect, but it was an intellect that was to operate within certain bounds. There could be said to be two types of knowledge: that known by the ratio and that known by the nous. The ratio is the deductive, logical, reasoning mind. The nous is what Orthodox Christianity still refers to as the 'heart-mind': it is a deeper level of thinking than mere reason, and it looks to attain wisdom: knowledge of the deeper truth of reality.

The same concept is called "the god-self" in some occult traditions, and it aligns somewhat with the knowledge spheres of the higher chakras in Hindu thought.

Most fascinating to me is the way esoteric Islam conceived of this irrational realm of knowledge: the "imaginal." The imaginal is difficult for us to understand if we think of imagination as something that is false, or the opposite of the "real," which wasn't originally the case in English. It wasn't until "real" took on extra connotations in relation to economics ("real estate," "realizing the value of your assets") that imagination became an antonym for the real.

Before that time, imagining something was understood to be the first step in bringing that thing into existence. Much like the way people now use the word "intention," imagination was a core ingredient in the work of magical change. The imaginal includes insight, intuition, and inspiration, and the more developed the imagination, the more actively a person can interact with those things as well.

It can be hard for us to think of imagination as anything other than something "made up" or false. What helped me is a trick I learned from one of John Michael Greer's books, a ritualistic meditative process in which you try to hold all the meanings of a phrase in mind at once.

Applying that process to the phrase "play make-believe" you get two meanings, initially. The first, and most obvious, refers to something children do—"pretending" or engaging in fantasy. The second meaning may take a while to unfold but changes everything, opening to many, many more meanings. I can't guide you through this—you must do it yourself—but start by teasing apart "make" and "believe," and remember that "play" is both a noun and a verb.

What's particularly fascinating about the esoteric Islamic concept of the imaginal is that it retains a degree of the polytheism that Christianity and Judaism scoured from their thinking. Because the imaginal isn't the realm of ideal forms, but rather the realm of potential forms, it doesn't fully agree with Plato and Aristotle, who laid down the foundation for monotheism. All human possibilities originate in the imaginal, all the worlds that can be manifested exist there. There is no "true" self in such a framework, but rather an infinite number of selves, each of which can become true. It's a bit like the modern "many worlds" theory proposed by some theorists of quantum physics.

The imaginal is irrational just as the nous is irrational, but unlike the nous the imaginal is an active realm of being in which we are created over and over again by our actions and our interactions. It's where we meet the gods, because they dwell both there and elsewhere, just as we do. We meet ideas there too, even though the imaginal isn't their realm, isn't the "ideal." But ideas live there, and are picked up like treasures to be manifested or like parasites to be spread.

The imaginal is the only way to escape from one way of being into another: You cannot become someone else until you can imagine yourself otherwise. I've always liked the phrase (attributed alternately to Mark Fisher, Frederick Jameson, and Slavoj Žižek), "It's easier to imagine the end of the world than the end of capitalism," because it unfolds in many ways when you apply the same meditative trick to it that I mentioned earlier.

Capitalism is itself a world that needs to end, and it's much easier to imagine the end than to try to imagine how we get to that end.

Therein lies the gate and the path. Look to the end, not all the stations along the way. If you get out at a station, you can remember that it's not your destination, not where you imagined yourself to be, not where the imaginal was leading you. Maybe you needed to stop for a bit, drop off some things you didn't need any more, wrestle with a few bits of a world you're leaving behind so that you can actually arrive in the next one.

That's all okay, more than okay. The imaginal requires agency because the imaginal is agency, but it also teaches agency, and so you don't need to learn this by yourself.

About

Rhyd Wildermuth is a druid, a theorist, and a writer on Paganism and politics. He lives in the Ardennes with his husband and writes From The Forests of Arduinna (rhyd.substack.com)

Other Titles by Rhyd Wildermuth

From Gods&Radicals Press
Your Face Is A Forest
A Kindness of Ravens
Witches In a Crumbling Empire
All That Is Sacred Is Profaned

From Ritona Press
The Provisioner
Being Pagan

From Repeater Books
Here Be Monsters

www.ingramcontent.com/pod-product-compliance
Ingram Content Group UK Ltd.
Pitfield, Milton Keynes, MK11 3LW, UK
UKHW021937190726
13853UKWH00004B/1504